You have heard the saying that someone is a legend in their own time. This is certainly a "truism" concerning Buck and Dottie Rambo. They have been in the forefront of gospel music for many years but they have also bridged over into many other music and religious communities. This book will be an inspiration to the young and all alike who follow the pioneering trail set forth by this now famous family.

Bishop Earl Paulk

Buck and Dottie have been dear friends for a long time and it's good to see their life's story in print. I know it will be a blessing to many.

Bill Gaither

Through the tears of hardship, pain, and sorrow comes the overpowering rays of hope, healing, and wholeness from the steadfast lives of Buck and Dottie Rambo.

Bob D'Andrea
Christian Television Network

The Rambos have displayed a unique strength in their ministry which I have admired through the years. It has indeed been my honor and privilege to perform Dottie's song "We Shall Behold Him." This family continues to be a great encouragement and inspiration to me.

Sandi Patti

Your heart will be in your throat as you live with the Rambos from farm to fame to faith learning the bride must wear combat boots.

Pastor Clifford Self
Anaheim, CA

I was eleven years old when my life was changed . . . musically that is. My mother took me to the Jones Hall in Houston, TX, to hear The Singing Rambos. It was my first experience with harmony that would make the angels envy. I immediately became a Rambo fan.

The Legacy of Buck and Dottie Rambo is a book every Rambo fan must read. It's also an important book for those who are considering going into the ministry. From their humble beginnings in the backwoods of Kentucky to their rise as "Christian music stars" to their valley of pain and sickness, the Rambos have learned what it means to follow Christ. It's comforting to read a book that shows two lives that have realized they don't have to have all of the "answers" to continue their journey.

As one great songwriter said, "through many dangers, toils and snares . . ." The Rambos continue to follow God wherever He leads.

Mark Lowry

No one in gospel music has inspired me anymore than the Rambos. I almost always shed some tears when I listen to their singing. This book is so inspired and speaks directly to the heart.

Barbara Spencer
The Spencers

This is a story of God's grace to develop "character" of His nature in two precious servants who have submitted the very life they live to "His Will." I am honored to recommend the reading of this book to all who honestly desire to walk in "His Character." **Lulu Roman**

The Legacy of Buck and Dottie Rambo is a story about music, the song and the psalmist. Here are two people who have touched all of our lives.

All the great songs that Dottie has written, I would have written myself—but I didn't know the words. **Larry Gatlin**

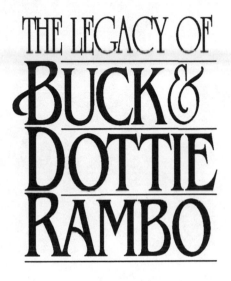

THE LEGACY OF
BUCK&
DOTTIE
RAMBO

THE LEGACY OF

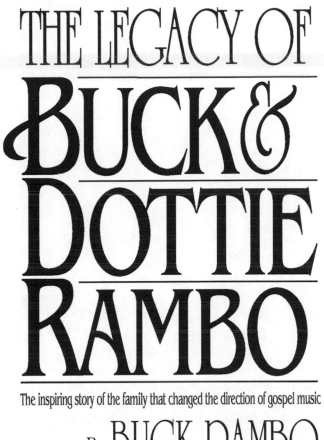

BUCK&
DOTTIE
RAMBO

The inspiring story of the family that changed the direction of gospel music

By BUCK RAMBO

As Told To BOB TERRELL

Star Song

PUBLISHING GROUP

Star Song Publishing Group, a division of Jubilee Communications, Inc. 2325
Crestmoor, Nashville, Tennessee 37215.

Library of Congress Catalog Card Number: 92-80758
ISBN 1-56233-041-1

Printed in the United States of America.
1 2 3 4 5 6 7 8 9 — 96 95 94 93 92

We dedicate this book to the legacy
we leave behind—

Reba, Dony,
Dionne, Destiny,
and *Israel.*

Contents

Foreword

A legacy is something one leaves behind to be handed down. Within the pages of this book, the legacy of Buck and Dottie Rambo is being passed on to the world, to everyone who will accept a part of it. It comes in several parts—in their singing, in Dottie's songwriting, and in the ministry of these two people to all who chose to listen.

Buck and Dottie didn't set out to revolutionize the world of gospel music. It just worked out that way. More than any other group, the Singing Rambos were responsible for swinging the emphasis in gospel music away from all-male quartets to family-oriented mixed groups.

There were already some mixed groups singing professionally when Buck and Dottie made their appearance on the scene, but those groups were a part of the establishment, so to speak. Buck and Dottie brought a new approach, a new sound, new instruments, and a new feeling to the business, and only then did it really begin to change.

Dottie Rambo is considered to be one of gospel music's all-time great songwriters, perhaps ranking with Bill Gaither as the top two. That talent like hers was bestowed on a little country girl who left home and went on the road singing in revivals at the age of twelve, is a tribute to humbleness. Dottie never abused her songwriting talent, always using it for the Glory of God's Kingdom.

Buck and Reba, the other two cogs in the Singing Rambos'

wheel, were equally as dedicated, equally as eager to serve the Lord. Combined with Dottie's alto, their singing set the gospel music world on fire.

Buck was the steady head of the Rambos. He took care of business while Dottie let her creative mind flow.

Their story is heartwarming, filled with all the elements that make a good novel, only in this instance they are true.

Bob Terrell
Asheville, North Carolina

Prologue

Did you ever ask God, "Why?" "What's going on?" "Where are you?" and a few choice phrases you would not dare admit even to your closest friend? Well, I've been there. I'm not proud of times of discouragement, or even times of weakness, but if you haven't been there, just thank God and pray it never happens to you.

As I watched the afternoon sun filter through the thick double panes of the hospital window, it cast a soft glow on the tired drawn face of my sleeping wife. In my own torment—the anguish that one feels as they helplessly watch a spouse suffer—this helpless feeling crept over me like a hot breeze and like countless times before, I questioned God and asked "Why?"

For twenty-eight days I had slept on the floor and did not leave the small hospital room in Nashville, Tennessee. It looked like the end of everything—our lives together and our ministry. How could we one day be on a mission field in the Caribbean and then wind up "seemingly overnight" in such a hopeless and dark place?

I guess this book is my search for the answer. Maybe if I go to the beginning of our story and sort through each phase of our lives, somewhere I can find out "What went wrong," or maybe the answer is "What were we doing right?" We seemingly were at the height of our ministry—writing great songs, making good records and seeing more souls saved and blessed than we had ever seen.

So in these next pages, please walk with me as I remember just how it was and maybe by the time we get to the end, we will have found some answers. At least the journey will be unforgettable.

CHAPTER 1

A Tough Beginning

"Little Dottie, get up and cook breakfast." Vernon Luttrell's voice came softly into the darkness of her room.

When her father called at four o'clock in the morning, eleven-year-old Dottie Luttrell snuggled deeper into the mattress of the warm feather bed for a last second of warmth. Then she eased out of bed, bare feet feeling the cold in the floor, and rushed to the kitchen where her father had a fire going in the wood-burning stove.

It seldom crossed her mind, but there were few girls her age who could get up at that time of morning when darkness still ruled Kentucky and cook a breakfast of bacon, eggs, cathead biscuits that almost floated off the plate, and sawmill gravy. Dottie had been doing that since she was seven or eight.

Born March 2, 1934, Dottie was one of eleven children, and while there were sisters older than she, her mom knew Dottie was the one she could depend on to get the menfolk off to work. Her mother, Elizabeth, was blind in one eye; her eyesight was so poor that she could not see well enough to cook, especially so early in the morning. The eyelid on her blind eye had been closed for forty years, and later, two years before Elizabeth died, we had her have a transplant, and she had 20-20 vision her last two years.

Dottie made short work of cooking breakfast, and when all the men had gone to work Dottie found an hour or two that became very special to her. While all the others were still asleep, she would slip into the back room where her brother J.B.'s guitar hung on a nail on the backside of the door.

World War II was raging on both sides of the globe, and J.B., her oldest brother with whom she was very close, had joined the Navy and was at that time listed as missing in action. He had given orders when he left—"Don't touch that guitar!"—but inside Dottie something was bursting to get out: She wanted to sing and play, and this became a tremendous desire for her, something she felt she *must* do, both to escape the drudgery of housework and to fulfill an urgency that was growing daily within her. The gift of music was born in Dottie and was burning to get out. She would go to her sister Nellie's house and Nellie showed her a couple of chords on the guitar that set Dottie on fire. She'd play Nellie's guitar until she had to go home, and when she got the chance she would sneak J.B.'s guitar down from its nail and practice the chords Nellie had taught her.

She would tune the radio to a country music station, keeping the volume low enough so it wouldn't interfere with the sleep of the others, and she'd sit and strum along with the music. Later, she admitted they were singing in "C" and she was playing in "D", but that didn't matter. She was playing! She was fulfilling her fantasy! Before long, she was playing well.

Several months later, J.B. surfaced alive and well, and when he came home on leave and learned of Dottie's desire to play the guitar, he was thrilled. "Sis," he said, "I'll get you a guitar." Dottie thought he would buy one, but when he got back to his ship, he made her a guitar. He didn't come home again for a year, but when he did he brought the guitar. She played the instrument for years, and it is now displayed in the Barbara Mandrell Hall of Fame in Nashville. It has always been and always will be one of Dottie's prized possessions. The first nickel she ever made singing is inside the guitar.

The Luttrell family lived on the army reservation at Camp
Breckenridge, Kentucky, near the town of Morganfield. Vernon,
known as Chick to his friends, was in charge of the labor force
of German prisoners of war, who did jobs of all sorts around the
base. Much of the time, there were POWs around the Luttrell
house, many of whom spoke fragmented English weighed with
thick German accents, and Dottie, never shy, conversed with
them. She learned early the heartbreak of war and the sorrow of
prisoners separated from home and family.

This was an exciting life for a little girl like Dottie. Camp
Breckenridge was a busy place. The government house in which
the Luttrell family lived was so near the gunnery and bombing
ranges that the family often had to leave home while maneuvers
were going on.

"We would come back home," Dottie said, "and our yard
would be dug full of foxholes."

When the army played war games, they were very real. Old
tanks, Jeeps, and airplanes were often used for targets. Dottie and
her brother Eddie found the wreck of a shot-up airplane not far
from their house, and for days they dragged airplane parts into
their barn and tried to piece the plane back together. They were
caught, however, and their toy taken away.

It was not at all unusual for military action of all sorts to take
place around the Luttrell house. Troops marched by, tanks rum-
bled up the road. Trucks, Jeeps, and assorted other vehicles came
by. There were rules as there always are at an army base, but some
rules could easily be bent, and before Dottie reached her twelfth
birthday, she learned to drive an army tank. What soldier could
resist such a cute young lady? And the Luttrell house was located
at such a distance from the army camp that no one was ever the
wiser.

"I had never driven anything," Dottie said, "but I just knew
I could drive. I got in a tank one day and looked it over and said
to myself, "I can drive this thing." The boys showed her what to
do and she got it going in circles and couldn't figure out how to
stop it. A while later she mastered the controls and could drive

it straight as an arrow. "Those soldiers were going ape," she said, laughing. "Imagine a little girl not much bigger than their fists driving that big tank!"

She learned most about driving, however, in an army Jeep. "Those soldiers would let me try anything," she said. "And it didn't take long to learn to drive a Jeep—stick shift and all."

She was a lot like her father, outgoing and forward. One afternoon she came home from school and someone had parked a car in their front yard and left the key in the ignition. Dottie hopped in, cranked the engine, put it in reverse and let out the clutch. She had never driven much in reverse and the car shot backward toward a high embankment that dropped from the Luttrell yard to the main road. When she hit the brake, it was a bit late. The car came to rest with its rear wheels on the brink of the embankment. Frightened out of her wits, Dottie ran the school bus down—two miles away—and the driver came back and got the car off the bank. No one was ever the wiser.

The Luttrell house was actually miles from the army camp itself, and Dottie enjoyed the solitude while growing up. She loved to be alone. A mile from the house, a clear stream ran through the woods, and on hot days she went there to wade in the cool water and simply sit for hours, listening to the silence of the forest. This became her favorite place.

Once while sitting beside the stream deep in reverie, a feeling she had not previously experienced came upon her. She began to sing a song. The song was not one she had heard before. It welled from deep within her, words and music of her own making. Never before had she been so thrilled. Immediately she ran home to tell her mother what had happened.

She sang the song for her mother, who began to weep, and finally her mother asked, "Now, Dottie, are you sure you didn't hear this song somewhere?"

"No, Mama! I only heard it inside."

Several years passed before Dottie realized that this was the beginning of a marvelous gift that would consume more and more of her.

The Luttrell family was a close one. Eleven children were born to the Luttrells. The oldest, Martha Dickerson, now lives in Phoenix, Arizona; and the others in order: Jerald Ben (J.B.) lives in Spartanburg, South Carolina; Nellie Slaton lives in Cedar Rapids, Iowa; Doris Hogan is deceased; Eddie is deceased; Dottie, who was born Joyce Reba; Lola Cornett lives in Killeen, Texas; twins Ebert Fay died at birth and Earl Ray died at five months; Jerry lives in Cedar Rapids; and Freddy, the youngest, lives in Morganfield, Kentucky, the only one who stayed near home.

CHAPTER 2

Influences

Dottie's life was deeply influenced by her grandfather, Isaiah Burton. Both of her grandfathers, Burton and Grandfather Edward Luttrell, were full-blooded Cherokee Indians. Both were from Kentucky, descendants of the Cherokees who were driven out of the North Carolina mountains along the Trail of Tears to Oklahoma. Some of them dropped off the trek along the way, and her grandfathers were descended from those who dropped off in Kentucky.

Grandfather Luttrell was a small, shy man, but to Dottie, Grandfather Burton seemed to be a giant. His deep voice and mild temper endeared him to everyone. Even Dottie's father admitted he liked having him around. Dottie could not begin to fathom her love for Grandfather Burton. When he came to visit, her whole world seemed to come alive.

She described him this way: "That's where I got my deep voice, from Grandpa Burton. I'm not one to idolize people, but if I ever had a hero, he was it. When I was a little girl, Grandpa fascinated me because he was so coordinated and such a handsome man. He looked like a big lumberjack, and he had worked in timber."

Burton had one problem that would have hindered many another man—he was blind. But it didn't slow him down. He was a fire and brimstone Baptist preacher, and when he began to speak, folks sat up and took notice.

He traveled from city to city, preaching and holding protracted revival meetings. Normally he traveled by bus, always carrying his white cane, but at times, perhaps when his purse was almost empty, he just stepped out on the road and hitched a ride.

Now and then he would come through Morganfield and stop and stay a while at the Luttrell house.

On Grandfather Burton's visits, after supper, Elizabeth, Dottie's mother, and Burton would sit at the kitchen table and listen while Dottie read the Bible to them. Grandpa occasionally stopped Dottie's reading to comment on a passage, and Dottie came to believe that Grandpa had memorized the entire Bible. Sometimes when she omitted a verse, or misread one, Grandpa would stop her and say, "Back up a little, Dottie; I think you missed it," and he would quote what she hadn't read.

One evening they sat at the kitchen table listening to Dottie read from the Book of Acts, and Grandpa suddenly started preaching. His voice filled the room, and his fervor reached a fever pitch. Elizabeth, normally a shy person, began to preach along with her father, and they were both filled with the Holy Spirit. A look of awe came over Dottie's face when the two of them began to speak in tongues, magnifying the works of the Lord.

That night, as she always did when Grandpa was there, Dottie climbed in at the foot of Grandpa's bed. He never let on that he knew she was there. This was Dottie's favorite time, for she knew that Grandpa would soon begin talking to the Lord.

His prayers always started the same: "Good evening, Lord. Ain't this been a fine day?" Then he would pray, calling out everyone's name individually and asking the Lord's blessing on them.

Dottie never heard him finish a prayer. Sleep would creep over her as she lay there engulfed in Grandpa's praying.

Just before Grandpa had his home-going, he called Dottie to

him, and placing a strong lumberjack arm around her, said, "Little Dottie, when you get old enough to know Jesus, make Him a good soldier." Turning to Elizabeth, then, he said, "Lift up my hands. I want to praise the Lord." He left this world praising and blessing his Redeemer.

By the time of Grandpa Burton's death, Dottie had become quite an accomplished guitarist and singer. She became so proficient on the guitar, and also in the development of her singing voice, that at the age of eleven she played lead guitar and sang with a Western band. "That was a long time ago," Dottie laughed. "I don't even remember the name of the band but I do remember that my mother let me go to all the places the band played except the dances. Any place there was liquor, Mom wouldn't let me go." Dottie became so well-known locally that she did a weekly show on the local radio station.

Dreams of becoming a country music star and singing on the Grand Ole Opry filled her head, but eventually, though she didn't realize it at the time, the impact that Grandpa Burton had made on her would dwarf her own ambitions. Soon she would face decisions that would affect not only her, but also millions who heard her story. Slowly, slowly, the influence of Grandpa Burton worked within Dottie.

The first person outside her family that Dottie ever saw play the guitar was an evangelist she heard on the radio. His name was Ernest—she can't remember his last name—and she talked her brother Eddie into dropping her at church so she could hear him. She sat in the back and was fascinated watching him play. And she learned from him by watching. She watched what chords he played and then went home and got down J.B.'s guitar and experimented until she accomplished the chords she had seen him play.

Music is born in some people. Some asked Dottie how she could play the guitar, not really knowing what she was doing, and she would respond, "Well, I hear it. I hear it in my head." Rhythmically they couldn't fool her because she was born with great rhythm in her.

She didn't stop with the guitar. She learned to play the steel guitar, though she thought that was a little tomboyish. Then she learned to pick the banjo, and began to play songs on the piano. "I couldn't play the piano much," she laughs, "just enough to run you out of the house." She mastered the mandolin.

People were fascinated to see a girl so young become so accomplished on the guitar, not to mention those other instruments.

Much of our personal strength is inherited. Strong people come from strong families. There are exceptions, of course, but this is the rule. Dottie inherited strength from more members of her family than her mother. Take her mother's sister, Dottie's Aunt Nora. She was a Kentucky midwife who delivered more than a thousand babies and never lost a one that was born alive. She was a fascinating woman, much into Indian culture. She raised her own herbs, with the help of her husband, Andy, whose thumb was entirely green. They also raised flowers, and their place was always a picture place of color. Beyond this, Aunt Nora's only vanity was her gold teeth. When she smiled, she looked like Fort Knox.

People came from all over the hills and hollows for Aunt Nora's poultices and potions. She worked by formula, and the formulas were handed from generation to generation by the Cherokees. She also raised goats to have goat's milk for babies who couldn't nurse from their mothers.

Dottie's mother was Aunt Nora's assistant in many of her deliveries. They worked as a team, and each knew exactly what to do. They didn't just take care of the mother and baby, but of the entire family.

Some of the families they worked among were extremely poor, and when time for a baby's delivery came, Aunt Nora and Dottie's mother would set out in a wagon, and in the wagon they would take enough food to cook for two or three days, or until the new mother got back on her feet.

They would take care of the daddy, too, who would usually be a nervous wreck, and would look out for the rest of the family's children during the time of their mother's incapacitation.

23

Aunt Nora was a fantastic seamstress, and when she went to deliver a baby to an extremely poor family, she shared much more than food. She always had a bolt of gingham or calico in the wagon, and while she waited for the birth of the baby she'd make clothes for the children.

Once Aunt Nora and Dottie's mother were getting ready to go back in the hills to deliver a baby, and Dottie's mother said, "We really should take some meat, but it's so far and they don't have any refrigeration, and I'm afraid the meat would spoil." Quickly, Aunt Nora whipped up a little pair of overalls for one of the family's children, stuffed a live chicken in them and tied them on the horse. "Let's go," she said. "We will kill the old red rooster and cook it."

She was creative and taught Dottie's mother how to make clothes patterns out of newspapers. Dottie's mother then passed this on to Dottie.

Aunt Nora was a champion fisherwoman. When no one else could catch a fish, she could. It was almost as if she conjured fish out of the river. And then she could make it taste wonderful, too. She knew more ways to cook a catfish than anyone in the country.

She was a strong woman, and no one dared cross her. Ninety-nine percent of the time she was right and she'd let those around her know it. But, looking in retrospect, considering the kind of life she lived and the things she did, the people she worked with, she had to be that way—strong and stubborn. A real pioneer woman. She was one who could have traveled in a covered wagon and survived, even thrived on it. Life was her adventure. She taught her kinfolk, Dottie included, to appreciate everything.

One day, Reba saw Aunt Nora down on her knees in the yard, still as a mouse, watching something on the ground that turned out, on closer inspection by Reba, to be an ant hill.

"Aunt Nora, what are you doing?" Reba asked.

"I'm watching this ant hill, honey," Aunt Nora explained. "You can learn from this."

She had a wide-eyed wonder about life.

Some folks didn't like it because she often used real mountain language of the strongest variety, but that was just Aunt Nora.

A notice telling of a local revival was not exactly earth-shattering news in Morganfield, Kentucky, because many evangelists made their way through that area. But it caught Dottie's eye, because the advertisement said the evangelist, Romey Woolsey, played the guitar and sang, and naturally she was attracted. The notice added that he was also blind but Dottie was accustomed to being around blind persons. Her mother was almost blind, and Grandpa Burton was blind.

But a blind guitar-playing preacher! This could be worth going to see, Dottie thought. She had no idea how much it would be worth to her.

She talked her brother Eddie into taking her to the small Pentecostal church on Saturday night to hear Romey Woolsey.

Romey played an electric guitar and sang into a microphone that hung around his neck and plugged into the guitar amp. Dottie sat spellbound, listening to him.

When Romey finished playing, another preacher began to preach, and Dottie responded to his message. He was an old-fashioned man who preached that folks who didn't change their ways and live for Jesus were bound for hell, and at the end he gave an invitation. He walked back to Dottie, and using her grandpa's phrase, said, "Little Dottie, won't you give your life to Jesus?"

Something came over Dottie at that moment, and she arose and walked down the aisle with him, knowing in her heart that she would never be the same again.

The following morning—Sunday—Dottie could hardly wait to tell her parents what had happened to her last night. When she told them, her mother sat and wept, but her father stormed out of the house.

That afternoon, Dottie was ready to be baptized in the Green River along with other converts from the meeting. The Reverends Hogan and Hatfield walked into the waist-deep waters of the river, and the new converts, holding hands, followed.

The customary thing was to sing a song and pray before the baptizing, and as the congregation stood on the banks singing and worshipping, so did those standing in the water, waiting to be baptized.

Everyone was so caught up in the moment that no one noticed Dottie floating off with the current. When Rev. Hatfield opened his eyes and saw Dottie drifting downstream, he quickly swam out and rescued her. The strange thing was, Dottie was so engrossed in the service she didn't know she was in danger of being swept away.

As the next few weeks passed, Dottie's faith in the Lord grew mightily, but so did her father's resentment of her commitment to Christ. One of Vernon's loves was coon hunting, and he loved to have Dottie sing when his coon-hunting buddies came over. But now her songs had changed: instead of the country songs she had sung before, she now sang about Christ, and this proved embarrassing to her father.

On several occasions, he forbade Dottie and Elizabeth to go to church. Dottie's mother would cry, but her father's ire only stirred Dottie's determination. Again she turned to her brother Eddie.

Eddie would park his pickup away from the house, and Dottie would go in her room, ostensibly to go to bed early, but she would swiftly change into her church-going clothes, climb out the bedroom window with her guitar, and Eddie would drive her to church. There Dottie would sing and play until midnight, and then Eddie would take her home and help her sneak back in her room.

Vernon caught her one night and made things rough for Dottie and her mother, and Dottie knew that soon she would have to make a choice between home and the church.

"I know my daddy loved me," Dottie said, "but he drank, and he was a high-stepper with women, and when I got saved he just couldn't handle it. He got rough with us, and especially when Mama and I were going to church, we caught it from him. I saw it was causing Mama trouble. He called me a Bapticostal because

I was part Baptist and part Pentecostal. He became mean to me, and during all those times Mama used to sneak me in and out of the window so Eddie could take me to church, I knew if Daddy caught me he'd whip me, and Mama would catch it, too."

CHAPTER 3

On the Road

Dottie's sincerity was evident in the way she lived and talked and sang about the Lord. More and more the people in the community and the church began to look upon her as a spokesperson for God.

Thus it was that at the end of a Sunday service, as he was dismissing the congregation, the pastor announced that "Little Dottie" would have the entire service on the following Sunday, and that she would "sing and preach."

The word *preach* always bothered Dottie. She preferred the word *speak* because it seemed more ladylike. But she had agreed to do the service, and she would, although she intended to tell the people simply of what the Lord had done for her. She didn't really consider that to be preaching.

At home after that service, Dottie's mother called Dottie into her bedroom. Removing her only good church dress from the closet, Elizabeth gave it to Dottie and told her to take it down to Aunt Nora and have her remake the dress to fit her.

Tearfully, Dottie took the dress, hopped on "Old Blue," the family horse, and rode him to Aunt Nora's house three or four miles away. Riding Old Blue wasn't an easy thing. He wanted to turn into every lane he passed, and Dottie would have to get off and lead him past the intersecting roads, and then climb back on again.

On the next Sunday evening, the church filled early, and by the time the service began there were as many standing in the churchyard as were sitting in the pews. Dottie stood in the altar and played her homemade guitar and sang for forty-five minutes. The audience loved it.

Then she laid down the guitar, opened the Bible and read a Scripture, and began telling of her love for Christ and His love for her. She painted beautiful word pictures and talked so affectionately of her Lord that at the end of the service there were few dry eyes in the crowd.

Her words moved several sinners to come forward and surrender themselves to Christ. Dottie watched with awe as the Holy Spirit changed these lives, and she realized there in the altar that this was her calling.

She knew, however, that the calling and her response were two different things. To accomplish such a task was beyond her ability.

A visiting pastor from Indianapolis came to Dottie after the service and asked if she could sing for a revival he was starting in his church. She was overwhelmed at the offer, but remembered that she must first ask her father. She promised to telephone the pastor with her answer and left to go home.

When Vernon heard Dottie tell of the invitation to Indianapolis, he became enraged, shouting and screaming, "No daughter of mine will be a holy roller preacher!"

He then dropped the biggest bombshell into Dottie's life that she had ever experienced.

"If this is what you want, young lady," he shouted, "you are no longer welcome in my home!"

She was only twelve, but Dottie truly felt the calling of the Lord. It was much clearer and stronger than the ties that bound her to her father. The saddest day of her young life came late that same week when Dottie's mother packed her meager belongings in a little cardboard suitcase that was almost falling apart, put a little tag with her name and address around Dottie's neck, walked the seven miles to town with her daughter, and put her on a Greyhound bus to Indianapolis.

That was the most touching scene of Dottie's life. She had no idea what was in store for her, but the excitement of being able to sing and talk of the saving power of Jesus to hundreds of people overwhelmed her.

Although she was only twelve, the day she left home was the day she began her full-time ministry for the Lord.

"That was the toughest thing I ever did," Dottie said, "but the greatest education I could have gotten. I look back and think, 'Lord, how would I have stood that if my child did it?' But I came from a family of eleven children, a poor family. My mom and I were the only Christians in the family."

On the road, she stayed in preachers' homes, going from one to another in time to begin a revival there.

"I came from good stock," Dottie said. "My grandfather and grandmother on my mother's side and my grandmother on my father's side were good, Christian people. My mother and grandfather put such a faith in God in me that I was never frightened traveling or in anything, really. I had some close calls with men, but the Lord always preserved me. He never allowed any molesting, but I had some close shaves. I was let down many times because I was so naive and so young I thought everybody who was under the cloak of Christianity was what they said they were, and some of the hardest licks I took in traveling was trying to get away from Christians who tried to molest me."

She was too young to drive, although she could drive very well if need be, but she always had traveling money because she was paid well for singing. She was paid by collection, and the money really was good. They took up a collection for her every night during a revival, and almost all the preachers were honest with her in those offerings—actually, more honest than some were during the early days of our singing after our marriage.

"They paid me honestly," Dottie said, "because I think they were afraid of God and thought they'd better give me what was mine. I look back now on those days with awe: I never sang to a house that was half full. They were all full. I'm sure I was something of an oddity—an attraction, if you will—because there were no other girls my age who traveled and played the guitar and sang."

She sent a lot of money home to her mother, and with a good bit of the rest she bought her mother things she had never had: her first washing machine, her first deep freeze, the first rug her mother had ever had on the floor. When she thought of something her mother needed, she bought it.

She had left home on blind faith. The only booking she had was the one in Indianapolis, but it turned out that that church was rather large, and the preacher had invited her to sing to a conference attended by a host of preachers. They liked her singing so well that many of them booked her for revivals and special engagements in their churches.

"Sometimes the meetings would last two or three weeks," Dottie said, "and I'd stay in one place—in the preacher's home—for that long."

She sang her own material. She had just begun to write songs at the time she started traveling. She sang them at the meetings and later recorded two of them.

"God gave me song lyrics that I could understand," she said, "and the people could understand them coming from a kid. They were what some people called Mickey Mouse songs, but they weren't Mickey Mouse to God and me. They were special. My gift was being developed. For almost every revival I wrote a new song, and teenagers flocked to the meetings. I was called a preacher, and I had a hard time with that. I never called myself a preacher. I thought of myself as being a teacher, and sometimes

I would say, 'I am a testimonier.' They'd say, 'How do you spell that?' and I would tease, 'I don't know; I made it up.'"—But it really was a word Dottie had made up.

"I sang, and I gave altar invitations and talked to the people who came forward, urging them to accept Christ in their hearts, and a lot of young people found the Lord. We didn't have drugs, and most kids left alcohol alone. The big deals were cigarettes and movies, and I didn't smoke or attend the movies. Our churches preached against movies."

She was a real traveler. She didn't just cover the country near home, but went to Texas, Ohio, Indiana, Illinois, Georgia. Word of mouth, preacher to preacher, got her the bookings, and when she came to a new town to sing, she usually found posters and handbills with her picture on them tacked up all over town, many of them stapled to telephone poles.

She carried her money with her, sometimes hundreds of dollars, and she was never afraid. After all, who would expect a tyke of a girl lugging a battered old suitcase and a guitar case to be carrying that kind of money?

"I never told a soul," she said, "but I hid my money in my guitar case. There was a little compartment in there for picks and things, and that's where I put my money. I thought it was safe there. When I got enough, I'd send it home to my mama. I shared with others, too. I loved to share with old people and little kids and sometimes I'd give money to preachers who didn't make good salaries in their churches. I didn't have anything to spend it on but Mom and clothes."

She bought a ton of clothes. Even at that early age, she recognized the importance of looking well-dressed when singing. Shoes especially attracted her. When we were married, she had two bushel baskets filled with shoes.

"Those were fun years," she said. "They taught me manners and things I carried over into my marriage. I met so many moms and dads who took my mother and daddy's places on the road that I felt I had a lot of places I could go back to. And I did.

When I would take a rest from the road, a few days or a week, there were two or three special places where I'd go back and stay with families I really liked."

CHAPTER 4

A Tom Sawyerish Bunch

Dawson Springs, the Rambos' hometown, was a sleepy little town on the banks of the Tradewater River in West Kentucky. Rising down near Hopkinsville, it flows northwestward to the Ohio River, and as it passes Dawson Springs, it separates Hopkins County from Caldwell County. Around World War II, both of those counties were dry, meaning no alcoholic beverages could be sold within their boundaries. But that was a joke. Numerous bootlegging joints did business in and around Dawson Springs, places where men could quench their thirst on the premises or buy a bottle and take it home. As a kid, I made money picking up empty whiskey bottles and selling them back to those joints.

Those who built and operated the whiskey dens were quite original in choosing the names of their businesses. There was The Goat Ranch, and The Block House, and the one I was especially fond of was The Floating Palace. This was a one-room house built on barrels and floated in the Tradewater River. The owners rigged the place to a strong line running across the river, and when the Hopkins County police came to bust the joint, those who operated it always knew when the hit would be made, and they simply pulled over to the Caldwell County side away from the Hopkins County jurisdiction. It worked the other way when the Caldwell County police made a raid.

Our family lived in the country, and almost every Saturday night I came to Dawson Springs and spent the night with my three cousins, Norman, Jimmy, and A.J. Sizemore. They lived in town, and their parents treated me like family.

We were a Tom Sawyerish bunch when we got together, and we had more fun than a barrel of monkeys. One Saturday night we all feigned an overwhelming tiredness and went to bed early, and as soon as we heard Aunt Cindy and Uncle Amos snoring—they always snored—we slipped out the back window and headed for the river.

The night was moonless and dark. Faint lights from town reflected on the river, but not enough to reveal our presence. We came down to the water at a point a hundred yards upstream from the Floating Palace, pulled off our clothes and slipped into the water, giggling and laughing at what we intended to do. We really made so much noise it's a wonder someone on board didn't hear us, but as we approached the houseboat, we were undetected.

This was in early summer and heavy rains had caused the swift water of the river to rise about six feet. A hundred yards below the boat was a dam.

As we came up to the boathouse, A.J. took his pocket knife, which he had clenched between his teeth, and cut the mooring line. The house immediately moved toward the dam.

We tried to swim back upriver but the current was so swift we could make no headway, so we quickly deadheaded across the river to the other bank. As we climbed out of the water, still giggling, we saw the boathouse nearing the dam, and those on board were vacating the premises in quick order, trying to jump to the shore and landing in the water, then thrashing their arms to get ashore, screaming and yelling.

Thank the Good Lord, they all made it off the boat and to the shore for the Floating Palace suddenly shuddered as it came upon the dam, then tilted its stern skyward, and crashed down the face of the dam, splintering into thousands of pieces and scattering itself on the waters of the Tradewater.

When we saw the houseboat go over the dam, we quickly ran upstream and swam back across to where we had hidden our clothing. Later, as we crept back in the house and to bed, we took a blood oath never to tell what we had done. No one ever found out who cut the rope—thank the Lord again—for those were dangerous men.

I've often thought about how we ridded Dawson Springs of one of its hellholes that night.

There was no place on earth like the Rambos' house on Sunday morning. Where else could you smell breakfast and Sunday dinner cooking at the same time? When Dad yelled, "Time to get up!" tiny feet hit the floor all over the house. Dad's name was Noah, and Mom's was Mary.

There were thirteen children in the Rambo family. I was born somewhere in the middle. In descending order, oldest to youngest, the children were: Margaret Pearl, Raymond, Benny, Amanell, June, Monroe, Mary, Richard (that's me), Hilda, Jackie, Donald, Douglas, and Ronald.

Mom lost her first baby, Margaret Pearl, only a few months after birth, and lost her last baby, Ronald, to pneumonia, an apparent inherent weakness in our family. Ronald's death was very tragic and left a great void in our lives.

Ronald was fifteen months old when he was found to be anemic. He was taken to the hospital in Evansville, Indiana, fifty or sixty miles from Dawson Springs, and in the hospital he grew very ill and developed pneumonia. Getting ready to give him a blood transfusion, a nurse prepping him made a mistake and gave him an adult enema and killed him.

We lived in poverty, so poor we couldn't afford a car, yet so rich in love that Ronald's death affected all of us for a long time. We buried him in the cemetery at our church about a mile from our house; and to show the extent of the love in our family, every afternoon when my father came in from work (he ran the laundry at the Veterans Administration Hospital in Dawson Springs), we would have supper, and then my Mom and Dad would walk the mile to the graveyard and stand around Ronald's grave and cry. Some folks said they could have understood it if Mom and Dad had had only the one child, but there were eleven left after Ronald died. Sometimes the whole family went to the cemetery for those late afternoon rituals, and sometimes the kids wouldn't go, but Mom and Dad went every day for two years. Then they went once or twice a week, and gradually reached the point where they went only periodically. Ronald's death struck them a hard blow, for they dearly loved their children.

I was born September 15, 1931, the eighth child. They named me Richard and gave me another name, but I don't tell anybody what it is.

When Ronald died, that left little Doug as the baby. He was born with Down's Syndrome and couldn't talk, but he was the center of attention in the Rambo family. Those who have never been around a Down's Syndrome child possibly cannot understand this, but the greatest love I've ever known, outside the love of Christ, comes through these gentle, special people.

Doug is in his fifties now, the oldest living Down's Syndrome child that we know. He has brought endless joy to our family. He's a chubby fellow and a very jolly person. Maybe an outsider would think him ugly, but he has such a beautiful spirit about him that if you could spend an hour with him he would steal your heart. Everybody in Dawson Springs loves Doug.

Doug always managed to entertain us. When he was about six years old, his favorite thing to do in all the world was to get outside and run. That was really great for him because mongoloid children have a tendency to become fat. He'd take a washrag outside with him and hold it up in one hand while he ran, and he'd get the biggest kick out of watching it stream out behind his hand.

While he was running, he would chase the chickens in the yard. He'd chase those chickens until they would finally stop out of sheer exhaustion. He would then walk away. He never tried to hurt them.

One day he was out in the back yard running and Mother

heard someone shooting down in the hollow behind the house. Suddenly Doug dashed in the house with blood running out of a hole in the side of his head. Mother grabbed him and examined him and discovered a similar bleeding hole on the other side of his head.

"Oh, my goodness!" she screamed. "Doug's been shot!"

Quickly she called the family physician and told him Doug had been shot, and the doctor jumped in his car and headed for our house at high speed.

Just before the doctor arrived, Mother examined Doug more closely and said, "That doesn't look like a gunshot wound."

Doug leaped up and began to grunt. He has never been able to talk. He ran out in the back yard, took a big fishing cane, and began to poke it under the back porch. The underpinning of our house was not closed in by a wall. There was about a four-foot open space beneath the floor.

In a moment Doug chased this big red rooster out from under the porch. Mother had noticed blood on the ground, and then she saw that the rooster's spurs were covered with blood.

Suddenly it dawned on Mother what had happened. The rooster had gotten mad at Doug for chasing the chickens, had hopped on top of Doug's head, and had sunk his spurs into his head.

She was horrified that she had told the doctor that Doug had been shot, and when the doctor arrived and learned what happened, he cleaned up Doug's wounds, laughing all the time, and wouldn't charge us a cent for the house call.

Benny, my oldest living brother since Raymond died around 1980, was single until he was sixty-five years old. When Mom died about thirteen years ago, that left Benny and Doug and Dad living in the house, and just before Dad died six years ago, Benny got married. He married a widow lady who moved in the house and fit right in. She loves Doug and treats him just like he was her own. The whole thing is one of the most beautiful love stories I've ever seen. They're like teenagers in love. She's one of the sweetest, kindest people in the world, and to see my brother, sixty-five years old and a grouch, fall totally in love with someone like that, was a tremendous experience for all of us.

All the rest of my brothers and sisters are married and have families, and most still live in Dawson Springs. We have a homecoming on the Fourth of July and everybody comes. It's quite a gathering.

Dottie talks of her childhood where eleven children lived in a thirteen-room house with a bath. I was born with thirteen kids in the family in a four-room house, and the biggest difference, I suppose, was that we had no running water or indoor bathroom. We drew water in buckets from an old-fashioned well in the backyard. Mama had no washing machine; so she used a big black kettle in the backyard which I would fill with water on wash day. I also chopped wood, built a fire under the kettle, and kept the fire going till Mama was finished. When the water came to a boil, Mom cut homemade lye soap into the pot, put the clothes in, and then stirred them with a wooden paddle, and the clothes boiled until they were clean.

We raised almost everything we ate. In the summertime, we all either mowed grass, tended the smaller children, worked in the huge garden, or helped with the canning six days a week.

It seemed that every time a visiting preacher came to preach in our country church, Walnut Grove Pentecostal, he stayed with us. Our family was the last one with an extra bed, or extra food, but Mama and Pop were so eager to help in the work of the Lord that many of us kids wound up sleeping on the floor and waiting for the second table to eat.

The old Walnut Grove schoolhouse I attended had only two rooms and two teachers—with an outhouse out back. Some of my fondest memories surround that old schoolhouse in which everyone was equal. I didn't know I was poor until I left this school and started high school.

I'll never forget what Dad told me when I finished the eighth grade and got ready for high school. He called me aside and said, "Son, that's as far as I can send you in school. If you want to go farther, I'll encourage you, but you'll have to pay your own way."

He wasn't being cruel, just honest; times were that hard, and he had a lot of mouths to feed.

Mom was a different story. She said, "Son, if you want to go on to school, I'll show you how."

In the summertime, I picked blackberries, and after Mom had canned her fifty gallons, I sold the rest I picked for ten cents a gallon. I also gathered scrap iron and Mom helped me get it to the junkyard. That's when I collected whiskey bottles and sold them to the bootleggers for five cents each.

Since I had to buy my own books in high school, I needed steadier employment; so I built myself a shoe shine box and shined shoes on the street for two years, putting myself through the first two years of high school. Then I got a job shining shoes in a barber shop for the last two years. It was an embarrassing job; but I was determined to graduate—and I did.

On graduation day, I felt so proud in my brand new $40 Stein-Mart suit and stiff new shoes that I had bought myself. At seventeen, I was determined to rise above the poverty that seemed to be everyone's fate in that small coal-mining Western Kentucky town.

In the back of my mind, however, was a nagging thought that I had gotten through high school by the skin of my teeth. My high school was a little country school, and World War II was raging. The principal and all the men teachers in that school had been drafted, and the school had to use teachers who had only a 12th grade education. That was the best the superintendent could do. I felt cheated, and I didn't even consider college because I knew if I went to a college that had a strong curriculum I couldn't make it.

Education, though, comes in a lot of forms. In one way I feel I'm very educated, and in some ways I guess I'm not. But if a person knows his limitations and stays within them, he'll get by. A person is stupid who doesn't know what his limitations are and won't admit he has them. I've been accused in gospel music of being a good businessman, but I've got sense enough to know where my limitations are and when I start to exceed them—I find someone who knows what I should be doing and let him do it for me.

I mentioned that my life was rather Tom Sawyerish, but perhaps a better description, with all of us kids around the house, would have been Waltonish. We were like the Waltons, only poorer. Yet, we struggled by and with some perks, too.

No matter how hard times were, if I couldn't manage to earn some money during the week, Mama, an all-knowing soul, was always there.

On Saturday, after all our chores were finished, we were allowed to go to town, and Mama had this unique way of letting me know I was her pet, that I was special among her thirteen kids. The pick of the litter, that was me! She would call me into the back room, get down her big, black, patent-leather purse, and count out eleven cents for me, so I could go to the Saturday afternoon movie. And if she had it, she'd slip an extra nickel to me for popcorn! Then she would whisper, "Don't tell the other kids I gave you this money. Just let it be our secret." And I swelled up like a turkey and left the house feeling really special.

It was not until I was grown and married that I found out she treated all her kids that same way. She could definitely teach you about the psychology of rearing children. She had only a third-grade education but she was some psychologist!

Mom was my best friend and I never had a secret from her. When I was about twelve and all the other boys were smoking, my mom took me aside one day and we had a heart-to-heart talk about the evils of cigarettes.

"Now, Son," Mom said, "I don't ever want you to smoke, but I can't control you beyond a certain age. I want to make a bargain with you. If you won't smoke till you're sixteen, I'll buy your cigarettes."

I was shocked. For a Pentecostal mother to tell her son that that was something else. But it worked. I never smoked a cigarette till I was sixteen, and I had such respect for my mother and father that when I did eventually start smoking, I never told them and I never smoked a cigarette in front of them.

It was true that almost everybody smoked back then—except

the Pentecostals and the Church of God, which is really Pentecostal. If you were a Pentecostal, you didn't drink whiskey or smoke cigarettes or chase women. Those things were taboo. But I suspect a few of the members disregarded some or all of these rules. A lot of people smoked, but this element of people preached terribly hard against it, and probably prevented some people from smoking. We all know smoking is a sin to our own bodies because it hurts the body. I know great Christians who do occasionally drink a glass of wine, and I know some who smoke, and I don't think it separates a person from God, but it isn't good for us. So whether it's a sin against God or not, it's not good for us.

I suppose the period of my childhood that is most memorable was that which took place as World War II raged around the globe. In the front window of our home hung a flag with seven stars on it, representing my three older brothers and four brothers-in-law who gallantly went off to war, leaving behind their wives and a family that loved them dearly.

It was a common thing for me to wake up late in the night and hear my mother and father praying, interceding with God for the safe return of their sons and sons-in-law. Their prayers were certainly answered. All seven of our servicemen returned home from the war safe and without a scratch.

I was just a teen-ager but I was the oldest boy left behind, and maybe this is what made me feel so close to my mother. She never stopped working. In the winter, she would always have a quilt hanging from the ceiling, and while she quilted, I would sit on the floor beside her and she would tell me story after story about being reared in a two-room log house with a dirt floor. Her father died when she was very small, and Mammy Lovell, her mother, would take in washing and ironing to put food on their table.

My mother told me many times about my great-great-grandfather who was killed by a bear, and she talked about how she became a Christian and Daddy threatened to come and drag her out of the church house. But she held on to God until Daddy was saved.

One of the things that worries me today is how children have lost the art of making their own fun. Toys were scarce in our house, but we knew how to play—and play we did! Every afternoon we would play till darkness drove us inside.

When Mom and Dad were away, I was in charge; and sometimes this was a real problem. My brother Jack was a character. One day when our parents were away, Jack went out and lay down in the road in front of our house and said he was going to let a car run over him. I thought he meant it and I physically dragged him out of the road. He was a mischievous boy, always getting in trouble.

One of my favorite sisters is Mary Agnes, and there is a reason for singling her out. One day we were digging fishing worms and she was digging with a four-pronged potato fork shaped like a hoe. Just as I reached over to pick up a worm, she hit me in the head and one of the prongs pierced my skull. I ran about twenty-five yards with the potato fork hanging from my head.

I was rushed to the doctor, who cleaned out the wound and sewed up the gash in my scalp. The doctor said I should go to the hospital and have a steel plate put in my head, but we had no money and couldn't afford such an operation. It turned out all right, and all my life when I did something dumb, I would explain by saying, "I'm not too smart; I've got a hole in my head."

From that day, Mary Agnes has kept me on a pedestal in her mind. She thinks I can do no wrong. As a child I must have taken advantage of her, because to this day I can mention the hole in my head and she will begin to cry.

CHAPTER 5

Marriage

A few weeks after my graduation from Charleston High School in Dawson Springs, my cousin Roenah Good stopped by with a special invitation for me to come to church Sunday night.

"They've got a good-looking Cherokee Indian girl named Dottie Luttrell who's going to start a revival," Roenah said. "You ought to come."

At first I hesitated, but curiosity got the best of me. Not too many new girls came trucking through Walnut Grove; so I thought I'd better check this one out. The thought that she was going to do a revival didn't scare me all that much. After all, I was a high school graduate and a pretty worldly fellow.

The revival was at a small country church in Rabbit Ridge, Kentucky, where my Aunt Flossie Good was pastor. Aunt Flossie was Roenah's mother. I slicked myself up for the occasion, and when I entered the church all eyes turned and stared at me. I was not exactly a household word in church attendance. Actually, I had quit going to church several years earlier because of conflicts within the church. I'm talking about conflicts within the membership, not theological conflicts. I probably wouldn't have known what theological conflicts were. These conflicts were occasional splits in the church, when part of the membership liked this preacher and the other part liked that one. My father stood against the faction that always found fault with the preacher, but eventually that faction split away and formed another church.

Another thing I didn't like about the church was its strict rules. It had rules that kids couldn't go to the movies, but my Mom sneaked me the money and let me go anyway. And it had rules that women couldn't cut their hair or wear makeup or jewelry, and boys couldn't play on the basketball team at school. If you were a member of the basketball team and got saved in the church revival, the first thing you had to do was resign from the team. I thought the rules were stupid, far too rigid, and I finally said, "I don't want anything to do with that," and quit going to church.

I should say at this point that the Rabbit Ridge church was one of those shouting, dancing in the spirit, aisle-running, emotional churches, the kind that made you feel uncomfortable just by being there. But when Dottie got up to sing, my heart skipped a beat—then another, and another. She wore a gorgeous blue satin dress, and her long black hair fell down her shoulders past her waist. When she sang, I thought I was listening to an angel. Then, she would pause in singing and play the guitar, and I had never seen a girl play the guitar before, at least not like Dottie played it.

Dottie said she had noticed me when I came in the church, and thought I was the cutest fellow she had ever seen. But I stood only five-feet, two-inches—the same as her height. She was fourteen by this time but looked and acted as if she were seventeen or eighteen, very mature. She called Roenah over and asked, "Who's that cute little guy sitting back there?"

"That's my cousin, Buck Rambo," Roenah said.

"Well, he's cute, but he's too short for me," Dottie said.

Roenah laughed. "I'll introduce you."

"No, don't," Dottie said. "He's too short."

So we missed that connection, but a year later Dottie returned to that same church in Rabbit Ridge and started another revival on the evening before Thanksgiving Day. Before the service began, she saw this tall, slender young man come in, and this time *her* heart missed a beat. She called Roenah over.

"Roenah, who in the world is that handsome dude sitting on the back seat?" she asked.

"Oh, him?" Roenah said. "He's the same guy you didn't want to meet last year."

In a year, I had gone from five-two to six-feet-two.

"My goodness!" Dottie exclaimed. "I believe this might be of God."

"Well, do you want to meet him now?" Roenah asked.

"Yeah, I sure do."

Roenah introduced us and after church I ventured, "How about going to get a Coke with me?"

"I don't know," Dottie hedged.

Roenah came to the rescue. "My boyfriend and I will go with you," she said. "It's just down the road."

That evening, the spark was struck between Dottie and me. We each felt that something unusual passed between us—a bond of sorts. Actually, I was going steady with another girl who was wearing my class ring, but when I drove Dottie back home that evening, I asked, "Do you have a date for Thanksgiving tomorrow?"

"No," she answered, "but I kinda like this little old boy back home, so I'm just going to be with Roenah tomorrow." She was hedging. She didn't have a boyfriend back home.

"Well," I said, "I have to be with my girlfriend tomorrow anyway."

But as I started to pull out of the driveway, I suddenly knew I wanted to see her the next day; so I stopped and stuck my head out the window and yelled to Dottie, "I'll pick you up about twelve." Then I drove away with my heart singing.

Roenah was with Dottie. She asked, "If you went with somebody tomorrow, who would you like to have a date with?"

Dottie answered, "He's the only one I'd have a date with. But he's kidding me."

I wasn't though. At noon the next day I pulled up at the house where Dottie was staying, and she went with me to get my class ring back from my girlfriend. Possibly I should say ex-girlfriend.

I took Dottie to my parents' house for lunch.

Afterward, I wanted to go steady with Dottie, but she wouldn't because I wasn't a Christian. She said she really liked me; she said I was "tough." And I surely liked her, but she wouldn't go with me.

I dreamed about her a lot after that, and soon she came to my home church for a revival, and in that meeting I found the Lord. Not because of her. I came under strong conviction and gave my life to the Lord.

My conversion was real, and she knew it. She consented to go with me then, and I was doubly happy. I had found the Lord and also had found Dottie. I thought my problems were over.

I took a job running a hoist on a small coal mine, pulling coal from the ground. For my labors, working outside in zero weather, I made the generous sum of one dollar an hour.

Dottie and I were seeing each other regularly and we were head over heels in love. I tried to save money, but couldn't—not on a dollar an hour—but I decided to buy Dottie a ring anyway. At a jewelry store in Madisonville, I bought her engagement ring for $67, and I paid it off $5 a week.

I couldn't wait to give Dottie the ring, but I had no way to get to Morganfield. So I talked my sister and brother-in-law, June and Melvin Baird, into driving me to Morganfield, about fifty miles away, in their old pickup truck, and there I gave Dottie the ring.

We all went to a restaurant for supper and afterward Dottie and I went out to the truck.

We were sitting under the street light, holding hands and hugging and kissing. She was wearing my class ring. I took her hand and said, "Dottie, I've decided I want my class ring back."

THUMP! Her heart hit the floor, but she recovered quickly. "That's all right," she flared. "I was fixing to give it back to you anyway."

"But I've got something else I want to give you," I said, and I slipped the class ring off her finger and put the engagement ring on.

47

From that point, things moved fast. Dottie's father had calmed down and was letting her come home for short visits between revivals. I moved to Evansville, Indiana, and got a job making Plymouth automobiles, and that surely beat pulling coal out of the ground for a living.

I reached the point that I thought everyone was working against us, from Dottie's father to several in the church who kept telling me I wasn't good enough to marry Dottie.

It was then that I made my first real promise to God. I recognized there was an anointing on Dottie that I had never seen before on anyone. She had a special gift, a special calling in life, and it would be difficult for Dottie to live a normal life. I promised God that if we got married, I would spend my life promoting and helping Dottie fulfill her calling, and I would never stand in her way in anything she felt God wanted her to do.

God must have agreed to that, because on July 1, 1950, in a Baptist preacher's home in Madisonville, we were married. Dottie was sixteen, and I was eighteen.

We went to the marriage license bureau and got the license. We couldn't afford a church wedding or anything like that, so we asked the man in the license bureau if he knew anybody who would marry us. He said, "Sure," and gave us this preacher's name—Robinson.

I telephoned him and asked if he would marry us.

He said, "Well, I've been ill, but if you'll come here to my home I'll marry you."

We drove to his home and he got out of bed and married us in his robe and pajamas.

I gave him $5. Today we'd say "Big deal." But $5 was a lot of money in 1950.

We moved into a one-bedroom efficiency attic apartment on Fairs Avenue in Evansville, and paid one week's rent in advance. That left us with exactly $12 to our name, but we were happily in love, and at that point money didn't matter a bit. Our apartment had no air conditioning, not even a fan, and we began to learn how to cope and manage.

In the next fifteen months, everything changed. The automobile factory I worked in moved from Evansville to St. Louis and I lost my job. We moved back to Dawson Springs, and I went to work managing Cavanaugh's Market, an independent supermarket, at $40 a week.

Dottie was much pregnant. She weighed 160 pounds. We made plans for the birth of the baby. We couldn't afford to have the baby in a hospital, but our doctor, Dr. Anderson, had a small clinic—just a few rooms in the back of his office—that he used as a place for birthings. He agreed to take care of Dottie through the pregnancy and deliver the baby for $75.

Dottie had a hard time in delivery. Reba was a breach baby, and when she was born on October 17, 1951, the marks of all the instruments the doctor used were visible. But in a few days the marks were no longer noticeable and she was beautiful.

The doctor told us that we could never have another child, but we felt so blessed that God had given us what we felt was the world's most perfect baby since Jesus.

We had never been people who believed in credit. If we didn't have money to buy, we didn't buy. About the only things Dottie and I have ever gone into debt for were houses and cars.

In the early days of our marriage we set aside enough money from our salaries for groceries, rent, and utilities, things that had to be paid. If any money was left over, we bought other things we needed, and if any was left after that, then we thought about going to a movie or something like that.

Once when Reba was a baby we miscalculated the amount of money we put aside for groceries for two weeks until we were paid again. For three days we had no money for food. We had enough baby food and milk for Reba, but all Dottie and I had were some dried beans. We ate them the first day and saved the bean soup, which we ate the second day. On the third day, the day before payday, we didn't have anything to eat, and we went hungry.

We could have bought groceries on credit, but we laughed off that thought and said, "We have to learn, and this is a good lesson for us."

That was the only time we ever went hungry in our lives, but we were relatively newly wed and we simply went about our business, feeling we had to learn to discipline ourselves better.

In one of our flush months in Evansville in 1957, we managed to save enough money to go to Nashville to one of Wally Fowler's All-Night Singings at Ryman Auditorium on a Friday night.

We had been to a concert before in Madisonville, paying our way in. The Speer Family was there, the Klaudt Indian Family, and Howard and Vestal Goodman were there singing with two of Howard's sisters. Dad Speer would stand on stage and sing and lift his hand and cry and it impressed me mightily.

So when we got to Ryman Auditorium and learned that the Harmoneers, the Statesmen, Blackwood Brothers, the Harvesters, and the Sons of Song were there, we thought we were in heaven.

The Sons of Song were completely different from the others. All the rest were all-male quartets with piano players. The Sons of Song were a trio using a piano. When they sang, it completely wiped that audience out. They were so good!—Calvin Newton, Bob Robinson, and Don Norman. They sang with such beautiful harmony that you never seemed to realize the piano was there. Actually, Bob Robinson played the piano beautifully, using it just to give them structure and keep them on pitch. We marveled at the way the three sang, how they swelled their words, and although they did not invert harmony like we did, what they were doing was akin to what we were trying to do.

We bought one of their albums, sat there listening until the singing ended at two A.M., then drove back to Evansville, about 130 miles, and spent the rest of the night listening to that album. Then I had to go to work.

That record probably affected our lives more than anything we'd ever done or known. We knew we could make it singing around the countryside in revivals, because we'd been doing it for years, but we didn't know we could make it as professional people in the concert world until we saw the Sons of Song. They made such an impact on us that we felt we could one day make it on the professional circuit.

Some of the members of the Sons of Song messed up their lives after that, but they are singing again today with the same enthusiasm they had many years ago. The Bible says, "The gifts and the calling of God are without repentence" (Rom. 11:29). The gift will always work. That's why a preacher or a singer's life can be all messed up, and he can preach or sing and it will still work because God still honors that gift.

Usually we didn't even have enough money to take in a movie. That probably saved us some embarrassment because the churches preached against movies. When Dottie and I had been married for only a few months, we went to see a movie in Evansville. It's strange what your mind will tell you is right and wrong. We went in the afternoon when we thought no one would see us, and you'd have thought we were robbing a bank. We looked up and down the street, darted to the ticket window and quickly bought our tickets, and hastened inside. There we sat on the back row so nobody in the theater would recognize us.

We felt that everybody in that theater knew who we were, and we got to feeling so bad about it that we got up and left before we saw all the picture.

That's how much I had changed in my thinking—or how much my thinking had been changed by the churches we attended.

I have laughed about that a lot in the years since, but it occurs to me that we allow people to condemn us. There are a lot of things in the movies today that we definitely shouldn't see, but back in those days what was wrong with the pictures of Roy Rogers, Gene Autry, Clark Gable, Katharine Hepburn, and people like that? Today, all Christians watch those old movies and enjoy them, but then they would have burned us in hell for it.

In our early years of traveling, the Baptists had one standard— one set of rules—and the Pentecostals had a set, and the Nazarenes had another set, and the other denominations had their rules, and here we were trying to work for God, trying to work churches, harnessed by all these rules and regulations that no one could sort out.

In certain churches they would ask Dottie to take off her wedding band before we sang, and she did for a while, but we became so disgusted with all the do's and don'ts that we began sending pictures of ourselves to churches, accompanying the pictures with notes that read, "This is what we look like, and if we can minister in your church and help your people, we'd like to, but this is what we're going to look like when we come."

Keeping up became difficult. One church would preach that a woman couldn't let her hair hang down, and another would preach that it was a sin for her to wear her hair up. Times were so difficult in that respect that not many people went on the gospel-singing evangelistic trail in the church world and lasted long. They usually became so disgusted with rituals and rules and regulations that they quit. Every church, it seemed, tried to change us into its own image.

But ninety percent of the very people who once asked me to resign from their church because my hair was too long and because we sang on television, now wear their hair longer than I did then and they all watch TV.

We went through an era when everything was a sin. A great move of God came about in the church world through the Jesus Movement when young people said, "Hey, we can do something on our own." Here came this bunch of long-haired people we called Hippies, or Jesus People, many of whom were real Christians who loved God, who held religious meetings without any ritual or pomp, and certainly without rules and regulations. At first the Church preached against them, but when so many things happened and thousands of young people found Christ, the Church eventually had to embrace those people. Rituals, the Church found, drive young people away. Today, many of those former hippies are pillars in the Church.

In many instances in those days, people did not want to become Christians until they reached their death beds because it took all the fun out of life. Today we teach people that the most fun they can have and the happiest they can be on this earth is by being born-again Christians. But back then you wanted to wait till you got one foot in the grave and the other on a banana peel, and just before you slid into Eternity on your death bed, you found the Lord. Churches today are aware of all that, and they have great youth movements, great musical groups that sing in the church and for the church, and it's all because they finally took the man-made things away and gave them some freedom.

Denominations are man-made. We are all in the flesh. We look for pastors who live what we feel we ought to live and can't, and we're always trying to look to someone who has had experiences we haven't had or a walk with God we haven't had, and when we find these people and get to be friends with them, and go golfing or fishing, we find they're just like we are. They have their own faults. There was only one perfect person who ever walked the earth, and He was the only perfect person who will ever walk the earth until Jesus gives us our glorified new bodies.

CHAPTER 6

Struggles

By the time of Reba's birth, we lived in a three-room apartment on the second floor above a restaurant. My brother Monroe, his wife Anna Jo, and their daughter Barbara lived in the
other apartment up there and we shared a bathroom. Our furniture consisted of a bedroom suite, a couch, a Warm Morning coal
stove for heating, and an old kerosene cook stove that dirtied the
kitchen so badly we had to wash down the walls every time we
used it. We had bought all of this used furniture for $75, and it
looked poor, but Dottie always made it feel special to us.

The day we brought Reba home from the clinic was grand and
glorious. You would have thought we lived in a palace; that's how
much the new baby brightened our home.

She brightened it so much that we began to feel expansive.
We decided to buy our first car. I had been given a raise in pay
to $45 a week, and I borrowed $225 from the Commercial Bank
of Dawson Springs when my brother-in-law, Melvin, signed the
note, and bought a 1941 Chevrolet. The people in that bank had
known me since birth, but the bank was so conservative it
wouldn't loan me the money without a co-signer. I repaid the

money in twenty-four easy payments. The bank people and I have laughed a lot about that loan in the years since.

That car was a pivotal point in our lives. From the time we bought it until we left full-time ministry, we missed very few nights singing and ministering somewhere. In those days, churches were always having revivals, and in that part of the country people began to expect that when their church had a revival, Buck and Dottie would be there singing.

We scrimped and saved money in every way to buy gas and go sing for revivals. Somehow, the thought that those churches should pay our expenses never dawned on anybody, and, Lord knows, I was too proud to ask. But we didn't care: We were in love with what we were doing.

Dottie had a special anointing when she sang and talked about the Lord. As she ministered, many times the altar would just fill up. We saw murderers, bootleggers, liars, and thieves literally run to the altar as she ministered under the anointing.

Dottie still played her homemade guitar. I had added an electric pickup and bought her a used Sears and Roebuck amplifier, but the guitar was shot.

One night, a friend, Walter Brown, who was not a Christian at that time, came to us after church and said he would lend us the money to buy Dottie a new guitar. Her need for one must have been apparent. The next day he and his wife took Dottie to Evansville and there she bought her first real guitar, a new electric Gibson, for $175. We thought we were in financial ruin, but in a matter of weeks people here and there just handed us enough money to pay for it.

Since that time Dottie has had many guitars, but not any of them ever made her face shine with such joy as the first night she played her new Gibson electric with dual pickups. From that time on, she could really strum.

CHAPTER 7

Call of the Lord

We felt the call of the Lord so deeply that I finally quit my job at the supermarket and we went on the road full-time. That was in 1953, and we had upgraded our automobile to a 1948 Plymouth. We loaded our clothes in Pet milk boxes and packed them in the car, wedging Reba in between all the stuff in the back seat, and took off. At the time, we had only one church booked, a church in Kingsport, Tennessee, but we had all the confidence in the world because we knew this was God's will for us.

On stage, Dottie was the star, and I backed her as well as I could, remaining in the background. I was so shy it took years for me to feel comfortable talking on stage. Still, God saw in us a faithfulness and a hunger, and He blessed us.

I had not yet learned to play the guitar, and when I learned it was in self defense, or necessity. We couldn't afford to hire someone to play the rhythm guitar, and we knew we needed a rhythm guitar to enhance Dottie's lead guitar. So, sitting around the house with Dottie, I learned to strum along. She showed me how to make a few chords and I began to watch her play more closely, and through observation, with her help, I learned to pick. Pretty soon I began to play around the house. She'd stop me when I did something wrong and show me how to do it right, and I began to get the hang of it.

For me, singing was worse than playing the guitar. I had sung when I was a kid, mostly congregational hymns, but once when I was seven or eight, I sang a little in youth revivals and things like that with my brother Monroe and my sister Mary Agnes.

So when Dottie first asked me to sing with her in our church, Walnut Grove Pentecostal, I didn't really relish the idea, but I didn't turn a deaf ear, either.

I could sing enough to harmonize with her, and we sang together at home, but I was shy and didn't really know whether I could sing with her in public. I had not been born in the pulpit like Dottie. She said she fell in love with my voice, and later she said I had one of the prettiest metropolitan country voices she had ever heard. Whatever that meant, I took it as a compliment. She kept begging me and finally I broke down and agreed to sing a song with her in church, provided it was an old hymn that I knew forward, backward, and inside-out.

She laughed and we picked out a hymn I knew well. We practiced until I was comfortable with it, and when we got up before the church to sing I was so nervous I felt petrified. My knees were knocking until I was sure everybody in the congregation could hear them rattling.

Dottie, though, was so calm it reassured me. We began to sing and our voices harmonized beautifully, I thought, and that helped to calm me, too.

But when we reached the second verse, for some reason she can't explain to this day, Dottie forgot the words. I had the book because she was playing the guitar, and she couldn't see the book, but forgetting the words didn't faze her in the least. She simply started making up her own words!

When I heard her singing strange words, I looked at her and she smiled and kept singing—and I lost my place. I couldn't find my place because she was singing words that weren't in the book, and I began to splutter and stutter and feel like a fool, and as soon as we finished singing the song, we went out of the altar and I told her bluntly: "Dottie, I will never sing another song with you as long as I live."

But that was like a lot of other statements I made along the way.

When we got to Kingsport to sing in that revival, we were dreaming of doing great works for the Lord. That was the only booking we had, and I had quit my job, and we could have been heading for disaster. But we had a strong faith in the Lord, and it helped. I wasn't playing the guitar yet, only singing harmony for Dottie.

Revivals then lasted for weeks, at least two or three weeks, and sometimes a good one went on for six or eight weeks. The one in Kingsport was scheduled for three weeks—so we knew we had a job that long.

Dottie did the talking. All I had to do was sing harmony. Reba was just a couple of years old, and we would sometimes stand her on the piano bench between us and let her sing a little.

All I had to do in the pulpit was sing harmony and help with Reba, and I was really beginning to feel comfortable. But when the revival was about a week old, the preacher threw me a curve.

Just after we finished singing and sat down, he came to the pulpit and said, "You know, folks, Buck's been here all week and we haven't heard him say a word; so we're going to ask him to come and give his testimony."

He didn't give me any way out. He just made the announcement and walked out of the pulpit and sat down.

I had never said anything in church. Hesitantly, I went to the microphone, looked at all those people, and said, "I praise the Lord for being here tonight, and pray for me I'll go all the way." I said it very fast, just blurting it out like a machine gun, and went back to my seat.

It had occurred to me that if we were going to make our living like this, I would have to learn to talk before people. I had a man-fearing spirit and I'd never done this before. I was scared. People may laugh at that, but probably most people wouldn't do much better than I did.

I resolved to overcome this deficiency, and the way I did it was this: The next time I was called on to testify, I said, "I praise the Lord for being here tonight, and pray for me that I'll go all the way and win somebody for the Lord." Each time I gave my testimony, I'd say the same thing and add a phrase. And then we reached the point that Dottie would pull on my coattail and tell me to shut up because I was talking too much.

"As hard as it was for me to get started talking," I told her, "don't ever stop me because I might never get started again."

In that way, I overcame my stage fright and became very comfortable before audiences.

We went from church to church, staying two to four weeks in each place, usually staying in pastors' homes, but often sleeping in church basements.

The most difficult time in our lives was Christmas because for years we didn't have a home—not a house, not an apartment. We were vagabonds who had nowhere to go but from revival to revival, and nobody wanted us for a revival at Christmastime. We'd have to go spend Christmas with either Dottie's parents or mine, and now and then there were some people along the road who'd become such good friends that we would spend Christmas with them. Those were hard times, especially for Reba.

We didn't know we were supposed to make money singing. That wasn't the reason we went into it. All we could think about was being out there doing what we thought we ought to be doing. That was the only reason we went.

A pastor once introduced us as "the fastest rising group in gospel music," and I thought, "Yeah, but it took us fifteen years to start to rise." Through the first ten years or so of our ministry, we averaged less than $50 a week in income. Money stretched farther then, that's true, but it didn't stretch that far because all the work we did was on the road, and to keep a man and his wife and daughter and an automobile running, and then buy food and clothing and all, really required more than $50 a week.

We continued to work churches, from one revival to the next, and a couple of things happened to us that made us realize the truth in our feeling that we were doing exactly what God wanted us to do. Both had to do with money.

We were coming in from a revival that had not been a financial success for us. I had to make a $100 car payment the day we got home and we didn't have the money. We didn't know what to do and we were talking and praying about the money on the way home.

When we reached home I opened the mail box and pulled out several pieces of mail. One, I noticed, was a letter from a young couple, Laura and Junior Helms, in Bloomfield, Indiana, with whom we had spent several of our vagabond Christmases. Quickly, I ripped open the envelope to see what they had to say, and in the letter they said they were praying and the Lord told them to send us $100. The money was in the envelope.

We praised God, for we knew that He had heard our prayer and answered it. Soon after that, Laura Helms was hit by a train and killed.

The second time the Lord showed us how He answered prayer was in De Quincy, Louisiana, after a revival. We sang for ten nights for a pastor named Bennett, an old bachelor about sixty-five years old. He was a godly man and had a good church. At that time I prided myself on being able to estimate about how much a church would pay us for singing, and as that revival wore on I began to realize that we could expect no more than $200 for this revival. That wasn't enough. I needed $400 because we had bills that had to be paid. I couldn't put off our creditors any longer.

I spent the last day or two of that revival praying, "Lord, I know this church is not going to pay us over two hundred dollars, but I've got to have four hundred, and I don't know who else to tell but You." I didn't mention it to anybody else.

The night the revival closed, the pastor called us into his office to pay us. He got out his checkbook and started to write the check. Suddenly he paused for about thirty seconds, staring away, and then he looked up at me and said, "Brother Buck, I was fixing to write this check for two hundred dollars, but the Lord just told me that you needed four hundred; so I'm going to write it for four hundred dollars if that is all right with you."

All right? It certainly was all right with me, and from that day until this one, nobody has been able to convince me that God doesn't hear us and is not concerned about us when we pray.

When I think about the hardship, especially what Reba and Dottie went through, it makes me weep. But, remember, God is faithful.

Still, the hardships were exacting. When Reba was ten years old, we lived in Kentucky and Dottie's mother stayed with us, keeping our house and sending Reba to school. Reba loved to stay with Elizabeth. "I loved to hear her read the Bible," Reba said. "She was almost blind, but she could read to me. She could also spin a yarn, and she told me wonderful stories about Biblical characters."

Dottie and I drove to Cape Girardeau, Missouri, for a one-night service and drove back home that night. All the lights in the house were on when we pulled in at three in the morning. Reba had had a touch of cold and we thought she had become worse. Indeed, she had. We found her deathly sick with a raging fever, and spots of blood visible all under her skin.

Elizabeth had been telling her the story of Samson and Delilah when Reba was suddenly hit with a terrible headache. Her temperature began to climb and Elizabeth gave her children's aspirin and bathed her with cool water.

Quickly, we phoned the doctor, and he said to rush her to the hospital emergency room. She was out of her head when we arrived at the hospital, and she called the doctor Samson and the nurse Delilah. Suddenly she began screaming, "Samson, don't let them cut your hair."

After several hours of testing, our doctor called in a half-dozen specialists who pored over Reba for a while in an isolated room. When they finished, they approached us in a crestfallen way and told us that Reba had spinal meningitis and had no more than thirty-six hours to live.

Nothing will crumble a person's world quicker than that. I became a basket case, lying across Reba's body crying.

Later, Reba recalled her walk into the Valley of Death. "Everything was dreamlike," she said. "I was on my back spinning, sinking into peace, and I thought it was the neatest feeling. Above my head was a light that began to spiral and I was going to the light. The light got brighter as I approached it—and suddenly I did a reverse spin—and the next thing I knew I was singing 'Oh, How I Love Jesus.'"

Our pastor, the Rev. Jimmie Russell, had come in. He had said immediately, "Reba will live and not die," and he had begun to pray. It seemed that a mist filled the room. Reba immediately awoke, raised up in bed, and started singing, "Oh, How I Love Jesus."

The doctors checked her again and found no symptoms of meningitis, and one doctor said softly, "The dead has come back to life!"

Those physicians who were in the room when Jimmie Russell prayed agreed that they had never seen anything like it.

The next thing Reba realized was how hungry she was. In a coma, she hadn't eaten for some time. She looked at Dottie and said, "Mother, if you don't fix me some beans and cornbread I'm going to die." She had never really known hunger until that moment.

Reba walked out of the hospital and never had another sign of meningitis. The only mark of illness was that her hair all came out because of the high fever she had run. Dottie calmed her when she discovered she was bald. "Honey, we'll pray, and it will grow back." She was right. It did.

Until this day, when any of those doctors see Reba, they call her the little miracle girl.

That episode had a profound effect on Reba's life. As she grew older she realized that God had given her a bonus, and she began to sense changes in her life. She began to feel that God had spared her for a reason, and that perhaps her life wasn't her own. She still didn't know what God wanted her to do, and still had it in her head that God wanted her to be a doctor and maybe go to Africa to be a medical missionary. But she definitely felt the touch of God's hand.

Jimmie Russell, our pastor in Madisonville, was a great strength to us many times in many different ways. He influenced our lives more than any other person. Not that I completely agreed with him doctrinally; there were a lot of doctrinal things we didn't agree on, but there was such an awesome anointing about him that you just knew this man really loved God and really loved you.

He wouldn't hesitate to tell you if you were doing something wrong, but he would tell you in such a way that you couldn't take offense.

Certainly he would stand by you, too. We hadn't seen him in years when Dottie got sick and went to the hospital in Nashville, but when he heard about her illness he drove to Nashville to see us.

Brother Jimmie was a godly man who had a strange quirk of wearing a white shirt buttoned at the collar, but he never wore a tie. He never preached against ties as ornamental or anything like that; he just didn't wear a tie.

He had a tremendous strength in faith, and an incredible belief in miracles and healing.

He came out of the coal mines, but it took him a long time to do it. He was a country boy who worked his way up to the position of superintendent in a big stripper pit company. He had worked for this company for years when he revealed that God had been dealing with him, wanting him to preach the gospel.

Like so many others, he resisted the call to the pulpit, until one day he fell in a coal bin with thousands of tons of coal moving through a chute. Suddenly he was covered with coal, moving through the bin. He felt doomed until he remembered how God had been dealing with him, and at that moment he told God that if he got out of that chute alive he would indeed preach. Miraculously, though completely covered with chunks of coal, large and small, he was swept through the chute and out the lower end with no more damage than a couple of scratches.

Jimmie Russell was a man of his word. He began to preach, and for a long time he extolled the gospel and worked at the mine simultaneously. During that time, he never accepted a penny for preaching. He made good money in the mines, and he was a giver rather than a taker. He would put his own money into his ministry, but would take none out.

The day came when Brother Jimmie quit the mines to devote full time to his ministry. He built a great church in Madisonville and called it The Lighthouse. It was Pentecostal.

Jimmie is from the old school, but is a very, very dignified-looking gentleman. If you walked into a room where he was you would feel his presence. You'd say, "This is a man of God." There is no question in anybody's mind in our part of the country that Jimmie Russell is a man of God. He's a good neighbor, too; if any one gets sick within twenty-five miles of him, they don't have to call him. He comes.

We all loved Jimmie Russell, and Reba especially had a special place in her heart for him. She thought the preacher in Dawson Springs was too strict. He was one of those who preached that women couldn't wear slacks, couldn't cut their hair or wear it up. They had to wear their hair down, and had to wear long sleeves. His church members could watch no television, no sports, no movies. Reba thought the whole church was based on you're-all-going-to-hell-if-you-don't-straighten-up-and-stay-that-way.

"We didn't hear much about the goodness of God," Reba said, and then she tempered her remarks and possibly her memory by adding: "I'm sure it wasn't as strict as I'm painting it, but these are the things I remember about it. They could make hell so real you could smell the smoke and feel the flames."

Jimmie Russell preached the goodness and faithfulness of God. His life wasn't just something you noticed in the pulpit; it was something you noticed every time you saw him, and something you felt the rest of the time.

Reba often spent the night with Jimmie's daughter, Suzie. Jimmie had a real knack for telling stories, and so did Reba. She was good at making up little stories, and they would sit around the fire swapping yarns. Jimmie never made her feel inferior, even as a child, with her dinky stories. He would sit and listen and encourage her. He made her feel special, and no doubt he had a great influence on her, particularly upon developing her talents.

We reached a point where we felt we could no longer sing full-time, and for a couple of years we worked only on weekends. We moved to a little town called Hebron, outside of Columbus, Ohio. I again took a job managing an independent supermarket and Dottie worked in a plastics factory, trying to regroup our finances and, really, our lives. Reba was in school. This was about 1957.

The store that hired me was in deep financial trouble and my job was to set it in order, turn it around, and make a profit for the company. When I took over the store, a representative of the company told me there was one employee I needed to fire. "He's an alcoholic," the man said, "and he and his wife are almost divorced." But before making any drastic moves, I suggested they let me work with everyone and make my own decisions.

Only a few days were required for me to find that the man in question, Bud Artz, was the best worker I had; so I kept him on the payroll and he continued to do good work.

For months, I worked seven days a week to turn the store around. Bud worked closely with me and soon became my right-hand man in the store. The tobacco companies and beer and wine distributors handed me cash money for shelf space and display space, and Bud seemed to be impressed when I rang this money into the cash register instead of pocketing it. The money wasn't mine to keep. By rights it belonged to the store, and so it went to the store. It helped to turn the operation around.

Each Thursday night Dottie and Reba and I had a little get-together in our home, attended by friends and neighbors. We sang and played and had a good time. Bud asked if he could come and bring his family. I told him, "Certainly you can, but you'll have to watch your language." Bud occasionally fouled the air with his swearing. He agreed to this, and he and his wife, Gerry, began attending. Bud no longer drank, and he and Gerry fit right in with the rest of the crowd. They became faithful in their attendance, and we could see them growing closer together again.

Sometime later, we were doing a Sunday service, ministering and singing, and at the end of the service Bud and Gerry surrendered their lives to the Lord and committed themselves to Him.

It wasn't long after that that the Lord spoke directly to me there in Hebron and told me to move to Kentucky and start a full-time music ministry. There haven't been many times in my life that I can say, "God said to me," but this was one of them. His was not an audible voice, but He made Himself known to me through an overwhelming urgency that came into my life, and I finally said, "This is what I've got to do." We moved to Madisonville, and that's when Jimmie Russell's daughter Judy came to sing with us.

This was around 1959. We couldn't just jump right into singing full-time; we had to work up to it gradually. I worked in a Madisonville supermarket to make a living, and we sang on weekends. Judy sang with us on our first recording.

Eventually, Bud and Gerry also moved to Nashville to be near us. They felt that God had sent the Rambos to their wilderness, which was Hebron, just to reach them. Dottie and I became godparents to their two children, Steve and Brenda. Gerry became our secretary, and Bud became my dearest friend.

We think our move to Hebron in the first place was mutually providential for us and the Artzes, resulting in their being saved and our reaping two of our finest friends and a loyal secretary, during those years.

CHAPTER 8

Jimmie Davis

One of the questions we are asked most is how we got our start in the world of professional gospel music. Of course, we give credit to the Lord, but also to a mortal man—Jimmie Davis, at that time governor of Louisiana and a fine gospel singer himself.

A year after we moved back to Kentucky, we were living in a house trailer behind Jimmie Russell's church in Madisonville, struggling along, trying to do the work we were called to do, but financially we were about as poor as church mice. Still, there was a determination in us that we should not stop trying to minister through song.

Jimmie Davis's singing career was at its height, and he, like all other gospel singers, constantly searched for good songs, not only songs to sing but to publish as well.

He and the Happy Goodman Family did a concert together and the Goodmans sang two of Dottie's songs, "There's Nothing That My God Can't Do" and "What Can I Offer the Lord?"

Gov. Davis went to the Goodmans after the concert and asked, "Who wrote those songs?"

Vestal Goodman answered, "A little girl in Kentucky. She and her husband work through the week and sing on weekends. Her name is Dottie Rambo."

"How can I get hold of her?" Davis asked.

We didn't have a telephone at the time but that didn't stop Gov. Davis. He traced us down at my parents' house on a Sunday afternoon. His secretary, a man named Chris, called. Dottie happened to answer the phone.

"Hello," said the secretary. "I'm calling for Governor Jimmie Davis, trying to reach Dottie Rambo. Is she there?"

Dottie was suspicious. "Yes," she said. "I'm here."

"I'm Governor Davis's secretary," Chris said.

Dottie laughed. She didn't believe a word of it. "Yes, and I'm the First Lady of the United States," she said.

They talked a couple of minutes and Chris said, "You don't believe me, do you?"

"No, sir, I don't." She thought someone was pulling a prank on her. Folks often did.

"The governor is trying to reach you about your songs," he said. "Where are you going to be tonight about eight?"

"I'll be at church."

"Do you mind telling me how to reach you there," he asked, "and I'll have the governor call you himself."

"Well," she hesitated, then told him, "I'm going to be at Madisonville at Brother Jimmie Russell's church, the Lighthouse Mission."

"Does Brother Russell have a phone? Could you be there at eight o'clock to answer the phone?"

"Yeah, he's got a phone." She gave him the number and hung up. When she told the rest of us what had happened, we all believed it but her. We encouraged her to be at the phone at eight o'clock.

It was a beautiful summer moonlight night, and Dottie and I walked down three houses from the church to the parsonage and sat on the back porch with the door open so we could hear the phone ring—if it did.

Suddenly, she began to cry. A strange, wonderful feeling came over her and she shed tears of joy. She said, "Lord, if this really is true, then let this be a door for our music. I don't know what to do with it. Just take it and use it."

Then the phone rang.

She answered. "Hello."

"Hello," said a familiar voice on the other end, "is this Dot, my girl?"

She knew the voice belonged to Jimmie Davis. She had heard him a thousand times singing "Suppertime" and "You Are My Sunshine." She loved his voice.

"I love your songs I've heard," the governor said. "Would you be interested in coming down to the mansion and singing some for me?"

Dottie was dumbfounded and speechless. Finally, she blurted, "I'd love that. I'd have to talk to my husband, but I'm sure we could do that."

"I'll send my private plane to pick you up," he said.

At that moment, Dottie felt like Minnie Pearl. She'd never been on an airplane. Not any of us had.

"Where can we land to pick you up?" he asked. "Where is the nearest landing field?"

Dottie asked me and I told her to tell him Evansville, Indiana.

"Can you get to Evansville?" he asked.

"Yeah, we can get there," she said, "but I still have to talk to my husband about this."

When she hung up, Dottie told me what he had said. That was on Sunday night and he wanted us to come down on Wednesday. I took over then because I handled the trio's business.

Dottie and Judy quickly began sewing on new things to wear. Dottie gathered up the songs she wanted to sing for the governor. Dottie paid $12 for a new pair of shoes. At the dime store she bought some beautiful material, light orchid, I remember, and she worked feverishly making dresses for herself and Judy. She didn't have a sewing machine and had to stitch everything by hand, and she did beautiful work. She and Judy looked great in their new dresses.

Dottie could take material she'd paid twenty-nine cents a yard for and make beautiful things. She always looked great. She could walk in a store and see a dress that would cost a fortune and say, "I think that would look good on me." Drawing a picture of the dress, she'd go buy inexpensive material for five or ten bucks and make an exact copy of the dress. Dottie made most of the dresses she and Reba wore on stage.

I went to J.C. Penney's and bought a sport coat on sale for $10, and all fitted out in this finery, we drove to Evansville and climbed aboard Gov. Davis's private airplane, a small, twin-engine craft manned by a pilot and co-pilot.

You could have raked our eyes off with a stick. When the pilot shoved the throttles open and lifted that plane into the air, we were aghast. Talk about a thrill!

Dottie was so thrilled she picked up everything she could find to save for souvenirs, even discarded chewing gum wrappers.

For some reason, I thought about Dottie's new shoes, and, knowing how well she liked to kick her shoes off, I remember cautioning her, "Dottie, please, when we get to the mansion, don't take your shoes off."

In Baton Rouge we were met with a limousine and driven to the governor's mansion. Not any of us had ever been in a limousine before. As governors' mansions usually are, this one was very plush. The things I remember most were the red elevator and butlers and maids everywhere. Our slightest wish was their command, but we had never even seen many butlers and maids, so we didn't really know how to avail ourselves of their services.

We were first shown to our rooms. Dottie and I had a huge bedroom and Judy had another. Sticking to our roles as hicks, we confiscated matchbook covers for souvenirs. This was unreal to us—a real Cinderella story coming true.

The governor quickly put us at such ease that within a few minutes we felt we had known him forever.

Dinner was at six at a huge table in the dining hall. Servants hovered around, serving us. It was a real treat!

The governor's wife, Alvern, was so gracious. She knew we were country folk out of our element, and both she and Jimmie made us feel so much at ease. Still, there were five forks at my plate and I had no idea which one to use. Where I came from we were lucky to get a spoon at suppertime. The food was simple, served in elegance. Except for the crayfish bisque, it was ordinary food, extremely well prepared. I had never eaten crayfish bisque, probably had never even heard of it.

When we went into the ballroom to sing for the governor and his wife, Mrs. Davis could see that Dottie's shoes were hurting her feet because Dottie stood first on one foot and then the other, playing the guitar and singing, and suddenly Mrs. Davis asked, "Dottie, would you like to take your shoes off?"

"Oh, I'd love to," Dottie said, and she always said she could see me turning red in the face, but Mrs. Davis put us all at ease when she said, "Well, I'll just take mine off, too."

We sang a while and then Jimmie came over and sang with us. He had a quartet called the Plainsmen, an extremely good all-male quartet, and they were there: Rusty Goodman, Thurman Bunch, Howard Welborn, Jack Mainord. They sang several songs, and then we all sang together in a jam session. It was great fun and everybody was at ease.

The following morning as we were getting ready to leave, Gov. Davis said to me, "Before you fly back to Evansville, I want you to come down to the Governor's office." When I reached his office, he quickly came to the point. He wanted us to assign so many songs to his publishing company, and when I agreed to do it, he began counting money into my hands. All of it was in hundred-dollar bills, and he counted out either $3,000 or $4,000. I had never seen that much money in my life. I don't know if I'd ever had more than $200 of my own money in my hands in my entire life. But as that pile of hundred-dollar bills grew, I knew right then that this was what I wanted to be involved in.

More than gaining a business partner, we had made new friends. When Mrs. Davis passed away, she left Dottie a huge brooch with matching emeralds, sapphires, and other jewels. Then Jimmie, no longer governor, would come to Kentucky and spend days at a time with us, and we had some real singing sessions with him. After a reasonable time had passed, we decided that Jimmie needed a companion. He was a very active man who needed a mate. We were also good friends with Anna Gordon, one of the Carter girls who sang with the Chuck Wagon Gang. Her husband, Howard Gordon, who had played guitar for the Gang, had died more than two years previously, and she was lonely, too.

Dottie and I arranged a dinner to bring Jimmie and Anna together. They had known each other a long time, had sung on the same program many times, and they quickly hit it off together.

Now making some money after Jimmie's contract gave us a start, we were singing in many new churches, and we moved to Nashville to get nearer the center of things. When Jimmie and Anna could get together, he would fly up to Nashville and she would come to our house, and they would court in our living room.

The subject of marriage came up later and Anna was reluctant but Jimmie was insistent. "We're not getting any younger," he said. "We don't have any time to waste."

She consented and agreed to marry him, and on December 9, 1969, we all drove together to Ringgold, Georgia, obtained the marriage license, and I performed the ceremony in a little Baptist church. We went to Ringgold because there was no waiting period there. We simply got the license and I married them. Also, neither Jimmie nor Anna wanted to make a big thing of their wedding. They issued no announcements, and made it a casual wedding—if a wedding can be called casual.

At this writing, they have been happily married for twenty-two years, and through those years they have become quite a singing team, appearing before thousands at major concerts across the country.

If God hadn't sent Jimmie Davis into our lives, the road probably would have been too rough for us. We are grateful to God for our friendship with Jimmie and Anna. They have meant much to us.

The meeting with Gov. Davis gave Dottie a new direction in her songwriting. Before, we had been singing her songs, and giving them to a few other groups, but now they were being published and made available to the world.

People who know the music business know you don't get rich off a gospel song. You begin to make royalties from it, but it takes an accumulation of good songs before you can make good money.

In the early days we got a penny for each of Dottie's songs that anyone put on an album—a penny an album. If a thousand albums were pressed, we made $10. And we got five cents for every piece of sheet music sold.

To start with, this amounted to just a few dollars. Then, as Dottie's published songs multiplied and became so popular, we got royalty checks for a few hundred dollars, and a couple of years after she began writing, the royalties went into the thousands of dollars.

A lot of time we'd be bogged down and didn't know how we were going to pay a bill and here would come a royalty check to drag us out of the hole.

I will say this—and it's the truth—we could not have survived working churches or concerts had it not been for Dottie's songwriting royalties. We have always paid our own way; we have always had to supplement our ministry from Dottie's royalties.

There was a period of about fifteen years that we took no money from the ministry. We put all the money back in the ministry and lived off royalties. That's a good feeling but is still almost an indictment of the Church. The reason that gospel groups have had to venture from the Church is because churches did not see the need to support gospel groups like they should have.

Gospel concerts, as we know them today, probably would never have come about had the Church understood what its obligation was to the gospel music world.

Dottie always said writing songs was like having children: sometimes they are premature, sometimes they are born quickly, and at other times she has to struggle to get one out. Some songs simply require more time and effort than others. She feels there are times when God makes her labor more over songs He wants the masses to hear.

"I found out early in life," Dottie said, "that seventy-five percent of my life was given to my gifts—my music and my writing—which left twenty-five percent for my family. I couldn't help that. I was addicted to songwriting and still am. It's strange how God sends songs to me. Some songs I've written in a few minutes, and some I've worked on two or three years. I wrote "We Shall Behold Him" in seven minutes."

Pat Carpenter was singing with us at that time, and Dottie and Pat were leaving the motel we were staying in to drive to a big tent pitched at the Baptist Church where we were guest singers at a conference. It was late in the afternoon and dusky dark. They were only seven minutes away from the tent, and Dottie hopped in the car under the steering wheel.

Dottie loves things like cloud formations, the ocean, and the mountains. Those are things that turn her on to songwriting. That day, as she pulled out of the motel parking lot, she looked up at the beautiful cloud formations and suddenly saw cherubs in the shape of the clouds.

When things like that happen to her, she usually begins to weep and laugh at the same time, and that's what she began doing then. A song began to come out of her, and she was trying to drive, weeping and laughing. She actually had a vision; she saw Christ coming through a path in the clouds, and heard the trumpet blast.

She didn't have a pencil or paper to write the song on, but God impressed it on her mind.

She said, "Patty, you'd better take the wheel."

Quickly, Patty slid beneath her and took over the driving.

"What's wrong?" Patty asked. "Are you sick?"

"No," Dottie laughed, "I'm not sick. Do you want to hear what the Lord just gave me?" And she sang the complete song for Patty, ending just as Patty turned the car into the church parking lot.

Most of the time when Dottie writes, she doesn't write just

one song; she writes several. I have seen her working on as many as twenty-five songs at once.

Dottie was not trained in songwriting, but she does know the ropes. She insists on proper meter, proper wording, correct English—especially correct English.

She always says, "God, I don't want to make You look bad," and she knuckles down on her grammar. If she doesn't think she has the right word, she'll search the dictionary until she makes sure.

An incident with the Speer Family years ago drilled the necessity for correct English into her head. She wrote a song titled "If That Isn't Love," and in it she wrote a line that read, "There's no stars in the sky . . ." and we recorded it that way. She said later that she just wasn't thinking, and when the Speer Family recorded it, Harold Lane changed the line to read correctly, "There're no stars in the sky. . . ." The Speers were too diplomatic to tell her that her English was incorrect, they simply corrected it and recorded the song.

When Dottie heard the Speer Family's recording, she said, "That's right! There *are* no stars in the sky." And, oh, how she wished she could have gone back and corrected it.

Since that time, she has been extremely careful about her grammar.

CHAPTER 9

The Gospel Echoes

We chose the name "Gospel Echoes" for our group in 1959. This came about because of a recording. Traveling and singing in churches only, we had always sung under the name of Buck and Dottie Rambo, but when we expanded to a trio and made our first recording, we had to have a name.

An association known as "Assemblies of the Lord Jesus Christ," which held youth rallies in various churches in Kentucky, designed a fundraising project, part of which was to do a gospel recording. We were approached about recording six songs on one side of the album, and another group would record the other side.

We agreed to do it, and the director asked the name of our group.

"We don't have a name," I said.

"You'll need one," he said. "Why don't you choose one?"

Judy liked the name "Echoes," but I thought we should use the word Gospel since we sang gospel music, so we settled on "Gospel Echoes," and that was the name we used until Reba joined us several years later.

We did the record and signed all rights to the Assemblies of the Lord Jesus Christ.

Our singing dates continued to multiply, and everywhere we went people asked us to make a record of our own. Other groups were doing well financially with recordings, but we just couldn't afford to make a record. We didn't have the money. I checked with a small recording company which agreed to bring its recording equipment to a church, make a custom record, and supply us with a thousand long-play albums for $600. But where could I get that kind of money? We were just managing to make ends meet.

We found again, as we had so many times before, that God supplies. A church agreed to lend us the money, and we made the album. Looking back, I would have to say it was a kind of Mickey Mouse recording, but God anointed it.

Never will I forget the day the truck backed up to our house and unloaded those recordings. I looked at the numerous boxes stacked on top of each other and thought, "I'll have records left when Jesus comes!"

Judy Russell was still singing with us. She was the first to sing with Dottie and me, making us a trio. But she fell in love with a young evangelist and married him; so we had to find a replacement. We hired a young girl named Shirley Bivins, who sang with us until Reba was old enough to join us.

After receiving that shipment of recordings, we loaded our clothes into the back seat of the car, filled the trunk with records, and took off for the Louisiana United Pentecostal Camp Meeting.

At the opening session of the camp meeting, we sang "The Old Country Church," and when we finished our stand, I announced, "We have our new album and after the service I'll be out at my car with them." When we left and I went to the car, a crowd followed, and within a few minutes I sold $1,700 worth of albums.

I thought I had died and gone to heaven! It was then I knew God had called us into the album-making business for two reasons: first, the money we made on the albums would help us stay on the road singing about the glories of God, and second, through the albums, God extended our ministry into people's homes—even the homes of strangers. What a glorious way to serve!

When that camp meeting ended, almost every United Pentecostal Church in the country was after us to sing at revivals. The Rev. Nathaniel Urshan, the church's Harvestime radio speaker, urged us to join the denomination so we could become their Harvestime radio singers.

Persuaded strongly by this newfound and wholly unaccustomed attention, I agreed to join, but Dottie never did, not because of any particular revelation but because she could not see any reason for both of us joining and paying dues. You see, we still had to scratch to make a living.

It is difficult for people who do not know the doctrine and persuasions of this particular group to understand what I am going to say. Remember, this was when Pentecostals and other denominations did not mix. This was when denominational churches, or non-pentecostals, were considered worldly churches.

Their teaching was then, and is now, that women cannot cut their hair and cannot wear makeup because *holiness is considered to be outward adorning.* And this included the length of sleeves. At the Louisiana United Pentecostal Camp Meeting, I went to the cafeteria to eat lunch one hot July day, wearing a short-sleeved shirt, and one of the church officials asked me to go back and put on a long-sleeved shirt.

Young people could not involve themselves in sports, and it was a very strict rule that "No Christian can have a television." A television antenna on a home was referred to as the devil's horns.

Actually, I could not understand this teaching, but I went along with it and eventually became as radical as the rest. For a time, I would not allow Reba to play with a hula-hoop. To me, it looked offensive.

The main doctrinal teaching of the United Pentecostals is that water baptism must be administered using the words "Jesus' name," or "In the name of the Lord Jesus Christ." This is based on Acts 2:38, which reads: "Then Peter said unto them, Repent, and be baptized every one of you in the name of Jesus Christ for the remission of sins, and ye shall receive the gift of the Holy Ghost."

Anyone who does not use this ceremony in baptism is invalid, and anyone using the ceremony "Father, Son, and Holy Ghost" is still a sinner.

Permit me to inject this into your thinking: I'm not condemning or justifying doctrinal teachings, nor am I speaking for or against this doctrine. I am trying to help you understand where we were, what we were being taught, and the circumstances that took place that almost wrecked and ruined our lives.

CHAPTER 10

Recordings

Time drifted on, and we made a couple of recordings for Warner Bros. Shirley Bivins had taken Judy Russell's place singing with us, and we had done two or three professional concerts in addition to all our work in churches. We sang one night with the Statesmen. Jake Hess and Big Chief Jim Wetherington had just worked out a deal with Warner Bros. to help them find writers and singers for a venture into gospel music.

Apparently Jake and Big Chief liked what they heard us do that night, for they talked to us after the concert about doing an album for Warner Bros. They told us we would have to sing Big Chief's songs on the album and that it would be entitled "The Gospel Echoes Sing the Songs of Big Chief Wetherington."

The only record we had ever done was that custom recording, and this sounded like big potatoes. We agreed—and the fun began.

Big Chief would send us songs on tape. He would strum a guitar and kind of hum the music into a tape recorder. His guitar playing left a lot to be desired, and his great bass voice wasn't the best humming voice around. We had a lot of trouble sorting out his songs.

When he sent us a tape, he would accompany it with a message that read, "Change these any way you want to."

Dottie would say, "Chief, some of these lyrics are pretty weak."

"Just change them," he'd return.

Dottie would redo his songs. She rewrote a majority of them, melody and all.

We made what I still consider to be a great album. It was so different from all others. Remember this was back in the days of quartet singing when the great professional groups numbered four singers and a pianist.

It was also at the time—in the late 1950s—when most of the big, affluent groups were beginning to travel about in buses rather than the long limousines they had ridden in before.

We couldn't afford a bus; we couldn't even afford to think of buying one. But we had worn out so many cars and were facing so much time on the road that we did buy a van, a Ford Econoline. After all, we were getting into the recording business seriously, and we needed better transportation.

We made room for our sound equipment and clothing in the rear of the van, and had enough room left over to make a seat for Reba. Then we had to decide where Dottie and Shirley would ride, and I fixed them a seat over the motor cowling.

The night we drove from Evansville to Nashville to make that Warner Bros. recording, the temperature hovered around zero. It was bone-freezing cold, and that van was so cold we had to wrap up in quilts to keep from freezing as we rolled along.

For this recording, we hired Brock Speer to play rhythm guitar and Ben Speer to play the bass. Marvin Hughes was on the piano and organ, and Charlie McCoy, who had just come to town, played the harmonica. We had a drummer whose name I don't remember.

The session was set up for six hours and we were to cut twelve songs. That gave us thirty minutes for each song, and that pushed things. Too, this was one of the first gospel recordings ever made with inverted harmony. The big male quartets had bass singers who sang bass, tenors who sang tenor, leads who sang lead, and so on, but we didn't work that way. When my part got too high for me, I switched to a lower part and one of the girls took over the high part. We switched harmony a lot and called it inverted.

We worked hard making that record, and the Warner Bros. people knew what they were doing. There was one problem: It was true that Warner Bros. gave us our first venture into professional recording, and we liked it, but when the album was completed, they didn't know what to do with it. But they liked it so much they wanted to do another recording immediately. Within six months, we went back to the studio and cut a second album for Warner Bros. and on this one we put four of Dottie's songs.

Warner Bros. knew how to make records but didn't know the gospel market. They didn't know how to sell our records. I truly think Warner Bros. came along before their time. The best album the Oak Ridge Boys ever made was one they cut for Warner Bros. titled "Folk-Minded Spirituals for Spiritual-Minded Folk." It was so unique and so good, but Warner didn't know what to do with it and it eventually died. So did our two recordings. They never paid off.

In those days there was no remixing, no overdubbing, and they didn't have stereo, but something called hi-fi.

All the people at Warner Bros. fell in love with Dottie's singing. They told us if we would agree to record folk—this was during the heyday of folk music—or country, they would give us any kind of contract we wanted. But we were so in love with what we were singing, we turned them down. We thought about the offer overnight, but refused it the next day and never looked back.

The Bible says, "Where your treasure is, there will be your heart also" (Matt. 6:21). Our treasure has never been with country music or soul or folk, but always with gospel.

In 1964 we signed a recording contract with the Benson Company in Nashville. We still lived in that house trailer in Madisonville, and I had to drive to Nashville every week or so. When I grew tired of making those trips, we decided to move to Nashville. I found a trailer park on Trinity Lane in Madison, rented a lot, and hauled our trailer down there with Mom and Dad crying that we were going to starve to death.

"Won't be anybody down there to watch out for you," Mom said, but a few years later, I got my Mom and Dad to Nashville and they saw the two new Cadillacs in the driveway of our antebellum home, beautifully furnished, and everything paid for, and Mom said, "Well, I guess I can quit praying for you now."

Those Warner Bros. records had been so good for us because we had learned how to prepare for a recording session, and when we went into the studio for Benson, we knew exactly what to do.

The Benson Company was the first to put orchestrations on gospel records, and the first one we did was an absolutely awesome thing. We had been used to singing with a couple of guitars and an accordion, and here sat a twenty-five-piece orchestra to play for these little hillbilly hicks.

It was a gorgeous experience for us. We put those big headphones on—first time for that—and found it easy to sing with those strings. That music inspired us so much that we captured an excitement on that recording that groups just didn't get in those days.

Benson was more a publishing company than a recording unit, and when we came, naturally they wanted to publish Dottie's songs. There was no reason not to let them do this, so we pulled away from Jimmie Davis's publishing house and put that business with Benson.

After a couple of years with Benson, we started our own publishing house. It seemed to me that Benson was not trying to push Dottie's music, but was simply putting her songs into sheet music and letting them sell themselves. People were beginning to pick up our songs off our records and recording them while Benson dragged its feet.

I thought the reason Benson wasn't trying to do much for us was because they were Nazarene and we were Pentecostal, and while no one said openly that that was a conflict, it really was. That was in the days when there was strain between denominations.

I told Gerry Artz I wanted her to come with us and start a publishing company. She asked, "What is that?" I explained that it was a company that published songs in sheet music and song-books and copyrighted songs.

She said, "I don't know anything about it, but I'll learn." She studied the publishing business and learned all she could about it. We didn't know much of what we were doing at first, but we had one huge plus: The first song we published was Dottie's "He Looked Beyond My Faults and Saw My Need," which raced to number one on many stations' charts and became in great demand.

We did our own distribution. I bought a house in Nashville and turned it into a warehouse and distribution center. We sold more printed music of Dottie's songs out of the basement of that house than the whole Benson Company sold with all their salesmen.

Basically, we sold by mail, but we also did some telephoning. We sold through established distributors like the Church of God in Cleveland, Tennessee. We automatically sent them a thousand copies of any song Dottie put in print, and that paid the cost of printing. So I had an automatic sale for everything Dottie wrote, and we were home free. Sheet music was big then, and we sold tons of it.

I eventually sold the Rambo Music Company to the Benson Company, and it now owns a majority of Dottie's songs. Jimmie Davis still has fifty or sixty of our songs, but Benson has far more than that.

Altogether, we figure Dottie has written about two thousand songs.

We were still holding revivals, mostly in United Pentecostal churches, and still living on about fifty dollars a week. Record sales supplemented this, but we used the money from them to get us into a better automobile and eventually to buy our own bus.

We shopped around among other groups and finally bought an old 1946 model Silverside bus from the Kingsmen Quartet. We thought we had finally arrived!

To let folks along the roads know who was passing by, we cut letters from plywood to spell "The Gospel Echoes" and attached them to the side of the bus. Thus prepared, we hopped on the bus and headed for Texas.

In Meridian, Mississippi, we came face to face with the reality of owning a big-shot bus: We blew the engine. It cost $2,500 to have the motor overhauled, and after negotiating a loan to pay for it, we resumed our merry way in a somewhat subdued mood.

There was something fascinating about that bus, even if it was a pile of junk. We grew to love it as much as any bus we ever owned.

Operating a bus is expensive. People look at you in a funny way when you tell them it costs more than a dollar a mile to operate a bus, not including what you have to pay a driver. We didn't mind paying it though, because riding a motorcoach was the only way we could keep our hectic schedule.

We graduated from that old Kingsmen bus to one the Chuck Wagon Gang sold us, and then to one the Klaudt Indian Family had owned, upgrading ourselves each time. But what a happy day it was when we boarded our first brand-new Silver Eagle and set out for our next concert! Equipped with a new Custom Coach interior and three private bedrooms, that new bus cost $69,000, but it was money well spent and money we could afford at the time. If we were to have a similar coach constructed today, the cost would be around $350,000. God was always there supplying our needs just as He had promised.

CHAPTER 11

The Singing Rambos

Shirley Bivins married a young evangelist, and we did a few revivals together, but I decided his goals and mine were definitely not the same; so we went our way and they continued in his ministry, which led them eventually to Florida to pastor a church.

We were desperately trying to find that third high voice, someone who could replace Shirley and hold up the quality of harmony we had attained. A young girl from Mobile, Alabama, Pat Green, was recommended to us. She was a superb musician, but she had great difficulty singing inverted harmony, and this was what we were best known for.

One night in rehearsal when Pat was having a difficult time, Reba, then thirteen years old, told her, "Here, Pat, let me show you," and Reba sang the part perfectly.

Pat was a tremendous instrumentalist who played piano, accordion, and bass, but her voice just wasn't high enough to blend. We realized with a shock that Reba's voice was perfect. Dottie was startled. I remember her saying, "Reba, I had no idea your voice had developed like that."

We had a concert with the Statesmen and the Happy Goodman Family coming up, and needed to put our act together quickly. Dottie asked Reba if she would be willing to sing with us until we could find someone who really fit.

To our amazement, Reba told us she wanted to sing. We all liked the idea of being on the road as a family, so we enrolled Reba in correspondence school, took her to a recording studio where we cut our first album together for Heartwarming Records, and she went on the road full-time with us.

That's when we changed the name of our group—in the late fall of 1964—from Gospel Echoes to The Singing Rambos.

Just as Dottie had grown up with music in her, Reba had grown up with music all around her. She thought everybody had pianos, guitars, mandolins, banjos, and dobros around the house because we always did. When Dottie and I weren't singing when Reba was a child, we had jam sessions at our house on Friday and Saturday nights. Here came the pickers and fiddlers. Dottie played about every stringed instrument, and I had learned to play the guitar rather well. So it was in that atmosphere that Reba grew up: There was always some kind of music going.

Having a mother for a writer, Reba soon discovered that nothing was sacred, not any little scrap of paper or cardboard. Any piece of paper could be written on. Those little pieces of white cardboard that come in panty hose were favored by Dottie. She liked to write lyrics on them, and when we began seeing all those little cardboard pieces lying around, we knew Dottie was writing.

In our house, we didn't dare throw any piece of paper away, especially if it had writing on it. An apparently abandoned brown paper bag might have the next hit written on it. Dottie didn't always have a tablet nearby, and when a lyric struck her, she grabbed whatever was handy and wrote on it.

Dottie had an ear for a phrase. Someone would say something and she would exclaim, "That's a great phrase," and would grab her little notebook or any piece of paper and start writing. She called the little notebooks "hook books" and kept them lying all around the house.

As a child, Reba learned to think and to listen that way. A thought, or even a word, might trigger a great song in Dottie's mind, and Reba picked up on that. Even as a child, without realizing it, she was going to a school for writers and singers. Her own ear was tuned to words, ideas, and concepts that would sing well.

She was so reared around harmony that when she was three years old, either Dottie or I said, "Let's sing something together," and Reba astounded us. When she joined in, she automatically went to harmony without realizing it. She had been harmonizing all her life and didn't know it. Music, harmony, lyrics, all of that was just a part of growing up. She thought everybody's mother played guitar.

Actually, Reba began her musical career by singing "When the Saints Go Marching In" on the radio when she was eighteen months old.

"I loved to sing as a child," Reba says. "I had a high voice like my grandmother Luttrell, my Mom's mother. Sometimes I think we grow up with luck. Mom sang alto and Dad sang lead, so the tenor as we called it was what was left—the harmony—and I grabbed it. Since necessity is the mother of invention, I just automatically sang the tenor."

Reba sang some with us from the time she was three until she started to school at six. God was very gracious to her as a child; he allowed her to see that Dottie and I had to sing; we had to be away from home. She always seemed to understand.

Reba explains: "They were gone so much they would sometimes stop and try to get jobs so they could be home more with me. Dad would work at a grocery store and Mom at a factory, and they were miserable. Finally, I was the one who would say, 'Get out of here; you're driving me nuts.' I really believe God gave me the gift of turning loose of my parents while I was young. I have talked to children whose mother and daddy were in the entertainment business or in the ministry, and they had great resentment, but before God I never did. I realized they had a call of

God in their lives that they had to fulfill, and that was the only way they would be happy."

Reba was a smart child. She came to recognize that there was a uniqueness about her mother that other mothers didn't have. And she often looked at me through critical eyes that gauged me correctly. She knew her mother was a creative person whose life was filled with hills and valleys, and she looked upon me as a steadier person who was a balance for Dottie. She felt I was the glue that held things together.

She once described it this way: "Mother has no business sense, and I don't mean that unkindly. That's the way with most creative people. She was always seeing to the gift of writing. She didn't know if we had five dollars or five thousand dollars. Dad protected her in a good way from that. There were times when I was aware of our low financial status, and Dad would share it with me, but there were things we kept from her just to keep her from worrying. Her gift didn't flow well when she worried."

As a little girl, Reba thought her mom was the most beautiful woman in the world. Dottie had thick black hair, olive skin, and almond-shaped eyes, and she was always so petite! There was a grace about Dottie and she exhibited it in a proud and graceful walk. She always smelled like heaven, and Reba found out later that Dottie would put perfume on little cotton balls and hide them in her bra. Then she would put the cotton balls in her lingerie chest. "There was nothing like being around her," Reba said. "She was the epitome of femininity."

Dottie was a fabulous housekeeper, and still is when she's well. Our house always smelled of Pine Sol® and Lysol®—clean to a fault. The house was immaculate, and even in the days when we had very little in the way of material things, Dottie made our home a thing of beauty. It always had clean curtains, slip covers, drapes, and bedspreads. She'd take wildflowers and arrange them beautifully. She could take a paint brush and make decorations out of almost nothing. And she could cook a meal with a minimum of ingredients. "When I came home from school," Reba said, "our house always smelled like peanut butter cookies, and there would always be something wonderful cooking, maybe rabbit stew or crackling cornbread—unusual things, but extremely tasty."

"It was a wonderful place to grow up," Reba said. "It smelled and looked like home. I didn't know we were poor till I was about ten, and I remember coming home from a Girl Scout meeting one day, riding in a van. We let all the other girls off first because our house was the last one, and after I'd seen what the other girls had, it dawned on me that we were poor. But I had never felt a sense of lack. We always seemed to have more than enough in our house, and we were always giving food and clothing away. Mother was always aware there were others in worse shape than we were."

Listen to what Reba has to say about me:

"My dad was the tallest man in the whole world," she said. "He's six-three but he seemed so much taller to me. He had thick, wavy hair that I loved, and he curled his lip when he grinned—a real boyish grin.

"He was an immaculate father. He and mother were well matched. He always wore ironed pajamas. I don't think I ever saw him in his underwear. He always looked neat, never unkempt. I don't remember seeing him with a stubble of beard on his face; he always looked as if he had just shaved, and he smelled like he had just stepped out of the shower. He wore starched blue jeans and his shoes were always shined. He was a proud man in that way."

Reba always thought the worst thing about me was how I was a stickler for religious matters years ago. "His convictions are very strong," Reba said. "He believed legalistic ideas so much: about women wearing makeup and such, that all of that was sinful. I don't fault him because he grew up with beliefs like that and he really believed them."

"I remember my dad and Grandfather Rambo getting into it one day," Reba said. "I was about eight and spent most of that summer with my grandparents while Mom and Dad traveled. That summer was extremely hot and my grandparents took me downtown and bought me a couple of pairs of Bermuda shorts and two little halter tops. I thought I was hot stuff. They also bought me a hula hoop. My dad didn't believe in anything like that. He believed your sleeves had to be to your wrists, and women couldn't wear slacks.

"When Mom and Dad came home, I was in the front yard playing with the hula hoop, wearing shorts and halter, and Dad came flying out of the car and charged toward me as if he were going to tan my hide. Grandpa came out and said, 'Okay, Bucky, if you're going to whip anybody, whip me. I bought 'em for her.' We laugh about that now, and there is no bitterness, because that's where Dad was then."

When Reba was in school she was supposed to wear gym uniforms for gym class, which included shorts. Several girls in her class wore their hair piled on top of their heads for religious reasons, and Reba had no such beliefs. Those girls were excused from gym class for religious reasons.

Before school began, Reba went to our family doctor, Dr. Fisher, for her school exam, and during the examination she broke down and began to cry.

"I can't go to my gym teacher and tell him I can't take gym for religious reasons," she wailed.

Dr. Fisher understood. "Well, we'll fix that," he said. "You've had a bit of a back problem—so I'm going to give you a medical excuse that you can't take gym."

She got to participate, keeping score and things like that, which made her feel much better than she would have felt sitting on the bleachers with the other religious holdouts watching the other girls exercise.

We didn't have a lot in the early years. Sometimes, we hardly had anything, but we had love. We talked. Our family wasn't the type that sat around watching TV. We read books, we played games together, and it was real family—and fun. When Dottie and I were home, the three of us had dinner together, and we had good friends in relationships that last to today.

Reba remembers the values we tried to instill in her. "I want the same things for my children," she says today. "I want tradition. I want Thanksgiving turkey. I want traditional values. I was raised with them and I appreciate them. Peppermint trees were a tradition in our home. One Christmas we hardly had money for a tree, and I begged Daddy for my own little Christmas tree. He went out and cut a big dead limb, painted it white, tied red ribbon on it, and hung peppermint canes and red apples and balls on it and put it in one of Mother's cannisters in my room. I thought that was the best thing I'd ever had, and peppermint trees are still a tradition after all these years."

The wonderful thing for Reba was that when she was small, we lived in Dawson Springs and she was surrounded by grandparents, aunts and uncles, and cousins. She never felt a sense of loss when Dottie and I were away because she had all this family around her. She also had an ability to go and fit in any of her relatives' houses.

Our families, both Dottie's and mine, were families that believed in work. We knew if we didn't work, we didn't eat. Reba was reared to believe in the same thing, and she has never been one to complain about having to work or simply to perform household tasks.

As she grew older—before she joined us in the trio—Reba didn't want to be a singer. Her concept of singing was having to sing in church and then sleep in the church basement, which Dottie and I had to do, and some of those evangelistic quarters in the church basements were slums.

Reba also began to note the strict beliefs and faiths, and in some instances the backward ideas of churches. If we had slick tires on our car, she noticed it when church members said, "Believe God that your tires and your gas will last until you get to the next place," and that's what we had to do.

But Reba thought, "I don't want to do this. I want to be a doctor, a surgeon." She had great love for the medical world, and still does.

From the time Reba was six until she was almost thirteen, she didn't really sing too much around us. She piddled around singing with a couple of her cousins, Barbara and Sandy Rambo, but she didn't really want to sing with us because she grew afraid that we would force her to leave her friends and go with us on the road.

She found new friends on the road. She was always at ease around the Speer Family because she and Susan Speer, daughter of Brock and Faye, were the same age and Reba was in the Speer home a lot in her childhood days.

"The way they dealt with their children impressed me so," Reba said of Faye and Brock. "Theirs was a godly home. Some people in gospel were one thing on stage and another backstage, but the Speers were always the same."

Reba had an unusual perception of herself—she felt awkward and a "loner." She always thought Dottie was one of those people who had all of her life together; she was multitalented, could make anything look good, could sew and cook, and Reba had a tough time finding her own place. She thought she was held together with safety pins and tape. She didn't inherit Dottie's hair, but mine, and it seemed to go every which way. She had big eyes and a nose that turned up so much she used to say she'd drown if it rained. She thought her mouth was too big. I suppose most young girls go through those stages, but Reba really felt like a left shoe.

She really had a misconception of herself. She was a cute little girl, very loveable, and she had a tough time finding her place because her talents had not yet developed.

Maude Aimee and Rex Humbard were big in Reba's life. We used to sing a lot at the Cathedral of Tomorrow. Once on a New Year's Eve, we were singing there and Reba had a high fever. "We were their special guests," Reba remembered. "They had that big stage that came up out of the floor, and we'd come up on it. I thought that was fun. But that evening I was sick as a dog and I remember Maude Aimee bathing me with cool rags and alcohol to get my fever down, and Rex was standing there praying over me. Their love, their tenderness, their gentleness, and their realness affected me. They were wonderful people, wonderful to me."

She continued, "To be around people like Oral Roberts, people who are so dedicated, was a great experience, a heritage that I don't take lightly. Mom and Pop Speer; oh, how I remember their goodness. Howard and Vestal Goodman and their daughter Vicki. I wouldn't take anything for those associations. We used to go from bus to bus. Like others would visit from home to home, we visited bus to bus. Mylon Lefevre and I were close growing up. We worked with the Lefevres a lot, and half of them were usually on our bus and half of us on theirs. Mylon is such a force with young people. He was a drug addict, and his life and recovery means so much to young people. Oral Roberts said he doesn't really trust anyone till he sees their scars. Well, I've known a lot of people who had battle scars. Big ones."

Tony Brown and Steve Sanders were good friends and still are.

Reba learned quickly that people who were not in the gospel music business had an unrealistic view of those who were. "They had ideas of glamor and things like that," Reba said, "and we weren't like that at all. We were quite normal kids. I remember Vestal Goodman had x-ray eyes, and I knew every time I was going to be around her I would be praying for God to forgive me for all my sins. Vestal had that way of looking right through you and seeing all, just like my mom did. I had such an admiration and love for Vestal."

Taking Reba on the road at the age of thirteen was a major step, but it wasn't the only key decision we made at the time.

When the album Reba cut with us was released, our songs were number one on most Christian radio stations, and it was then that I made the decision that would forever change the course of our ministry.

We were invited to sing on television! The invitation came from the syndicated show, *Gospel Singing Jubilee*, which was a major production seen coast to coast. Playing for time, we delayed making a decision until I could talk with the elders of the church.

The General Conference of the United Pentecostal Churches gathered soon after that in Grand Rapids, Michigan, and there I met with eight ministers whom I considered to be my best preacher friends, men who would honestly and correctly advise me what to do. Remember, the Pentecostal rule was that no one in the church could have a television set. But, oddly, there was no church rule against appearing on television.

All eight preachers advised me to accept the TV offer, and one even commented, "I don't see anything wrong with putting clean water down a dirty sewer!"

So the next week we went to Nashville as special guests on the *Gospel Singing Jubilee*. We sang with the Florida Boys, the Happy Goodman Family, and the Dixie Echoes, and it was a wonderful experience. They all applauded our singing and we were so excited.

Little did I know the fate that awaited.

As soon as the television show aired for the first time with us singing on it, my telephone began to ring. The same men who had advised me to go on television called and cancelled all our meetings. Other churches did the same.

Some United Pentecostal churches had Rambo record-burning parties in which all church members brought their Rambo records and threw them into a bonfire.

We were openly condemned and blackballed from pulpits, and their reasoning was that no Christian would display his ministry before the world on television!

These were my spiritual elders and fathers. I was so devastated

Gospel Music Hall of Fame

To all to whom these presents may come Greetings be it known now and for time immemorial that the conferring of this honor is the highest tribute to mortal accomplishment in the field of gospel music and yet, it is but a grain in the sands of time and the presence of God.

The members and friends of the gospel music industry and the Board of Directors and membership of the Gospel Music Association do hereby pay tribute to the accomplishments and spirit of selfless dedication that have touched the lives of millions through the spreading of the True Word and the Good News.

Whereas, there has been established by the Gospel Music Association an institution devoted to recognizing and honoring those few bright lights who have illuminated the paths of millions through their music; and

Whereas, by action of the President and Chairman of the Board of Directors of the Gospel Music Association and by action of the Hall of Fame Committee the Hall of Fame electors, the general membership of the Gospel Music Association and friends of gospel music everywhere; and

Whereas, this great light of gospel music has been judged by peers on earth to be worthy of memorial recognition by reason of indelible impact on the annals of gospel history; and

Whereas, this great light has evidenced the qualities of accomplishment necessary to obtain the approbation of the Grand Architect of the Universe with regard to gospel activity, influence in time or significance and selfless devotion, both in professional and personal life;

Know Ye that we, pursuant to an act of our assembled bodies do hereby invite, admit and induct

Dottie Rambo

into the membership of the Gospel Music Hall of Fame to share in all rights and privileges appertaining thereto; and

In testimony whereof, we have caused these names to be made patent and our great seal to be hereunto affixed the sixth day of April in the 216th year of our independence and in the year of our Lord, Nineteen Hundred and ninety-two.

Dottie's induction into the Gospel Music Hall of Fame April 6, 1992

Dottie at 16 years old

Buck at 18 years old

Reba about age 3

Brothers Monroe and Buck

Dottie age 12 with a friend

Dottie and Katie

Dottie and her Honda

Buck, Dottie, and Reba

Shirley Bivins, Buck, and Dottie

"Gospel Echoes" Buck, Judy Russell, and Dottie

Buck, Reba, and Dottie

Buck, Pat Jones, Reba, and Dottie

Doing a telethon for The 700 Club

In Concert

The Rambos

The Rambos with Kenny Parker

The Rambos with Kenny Parker

The Rambos

The Rambos

Dottie, Buck, Patty Carpenter

Rambos with our band *The Sonshine Express*. L to R: Johnny,
Wendell, Reba, Buck, Dottie, Bee, Jackie, and Ernie

Rambos on the Grand Ole Opry

"Charitys Children"
Judy Sproles, Reba,
and Tony Brown

Buck, Dottie, Reba, and Dony

Our Grandkids Israel, Dionne, and Destiny

Destiny McGuire

Israel McGuire

Dionne McGuire Gardner

My brother, Doug

Our parents Noah and Mary Rambo, Elizabeth and Vernon Luttrell

Dony and Reba McGuire

Dony and Reba McGuire

Buck Rambo

Dottie Rambo

Buck and Dottie

I thought my life was over. No churches to sing in! What were we to do?

It was my actual belief at that time that there was no church outside the United Pentecostal Church.

CHAPTER 12

Our Big Boost

We wondered how we would survive. Almost all of our working schedule had been in United Pentecostal churches, and now we were denied that forum. Our horizons were dim; we didn't know which way to turn.

In the sixties, there was one thing that separated the professional gospel singer from the nonprofessional: the National Quartet Convention. Contrary to what you may have heard, it was not just for Southern Gospel Music. That title was conjured when some groups took it upon themselves to call their style of music "contemporary," and in retaliation other groups came up with the title of "Southern Gospel Music."

In 1964, we were singing at a revival in Memphis at the time the National Quartet Convention was going on in Ellis Auditorium. Several people at the revival thought we were good enough to sing at the convention and decided to see if they couldn't get us on.

Jack Campbell had written a song titled "Jesus" and we were singing it. It was a good song, very stirring, and people responded to it.

There was one stumbling block: the National Quartet Convention was for quartets. They did not allow trios, duets, or solos on the program. But a friend who had pull with J. D. Sumner and James Blackwood, who ran the convention, talked them into listening to us sing, and when they did, they gave us a place on the program.

I had rented a booth the first day of the convention and we had our three records displayed for sale, that first custom record and the two Warner Bros. records.

J.D. came to our booth.

"I never heard of the Gospel Echoes," he said in his deepest bass voice. "Who are you?"

We told him who we were.

"Well, we don't let anybody sing here that's not professional," he said. "You just sing at churches."

We had done some concerts and told him so. We had sung with the Statesmen and the Happy Goodman Family, and various others.

"I'll tell you what we're gonna do," J.D. said. "We're gonna let you go out and sing two songs. Don't talk. Don't preach. Just sing."

That's all we wanted to do. The time slot they gave us was not a very good one, but we didn't know that. Time slots don't matter to God; He has a time for everything.

Dottie had just written "He Looked Beyond My Faults and Saw My Need." I introduced the group on stage, and we began to sing "Jesus," and the crowd really got with it. Then we started singing "He Looked Beyond My Faults" and the anointing came over us. The crowd came to its feet, clapping and cheering, and it seemed they stood there forever. It swept us off our feet; we weren't expecting anything like that. That crowd literally came unglued. People shouted and ran the aisles, and we had to keep singing, and finally J.D. and James came on stage and started singing with us. We had to sing the song so long they had learned it!

The glory of the Lord filled the place! Gospel promoters from all over the nation were there, and through the next few months, we received many bookings on the professional concert circuit. We couldn't take all of them because we were still singing in churches. Before I knew it, the concert world had picked up the pieces of our shattered careers and we had the opportunity to grow stronger and larger than we had ever been. Promoters like W.B. Nowlin in Texas and Lloyd Orrell up North used us constantly as a fill-in group and paid us a hundred or a hundred-fifty dollars for each appearance. The money began to add up, and we got on our feet.

Our music on stage was Dottie's guitar and Shirley's accordion. Right after that was when I started playing rhythm guitar on stage, and when Reba came with us later that fall she started playing bass.

At the time, during male quartet days, it was unheard-of that three people could walk out there with a guitar and tear the walls down, especially when two of the three were women. But things skyrocketed for us. The National Quartet Convention launched us onto the concert circuit, and we started doing television just after that.

The Lord was definitely working on us. We were invited to sing at the First Assembly of God in Lakeland, Florida, where the Rev. Karl Strader was pastor. After we sang, Rev. Strader preached the greatest sermon I have ever heard on the Godhead and the name of Jesus.

Piece by piece, he peeled off my layers of religious prejudice, and I saw immediately that God's Church transcended denominational barriers and personal theology.

He helped me to see that God's Church encompasses everyone who is born again.

From that day forward, I have never had a problem with theology. I love the Baptists, and I love the Nazarenes. I love all denominational people.

And I truly believe that from that day on, no church could say that the Rambos did anything but good, and that the Rambos were anything but a blessing in their church.

As if to put a finishing touch to this story, when we sang next in Monroe, Louisiana, the Rev. A. T. Morgan, general superintendent of the United Pentecostal Church, came to see us and openly repented for the way the United Pentecostal churches had mistreated us.

About a month later, Rev. Morgan asked us to stop by his home in DeRidder, Louisiana, and visit with him. We accepted his invitation, and when we started to leave, again he said, "Brother and Sister Rambo, I must make sure there is nothing between you and me. Please forgive us of our ignorance. I have come to realize that television is the greatest tool God has ever given to preach the Gospel. Use it. Take your message to any church that will receive it."

Then he laid his hands on us in the most awesome moving of the Holy Spirit, prophesying over us that our ministry would affect the world.

Only a few days later, Rev. Morgan went home to be with the Lord.

CHAPTER 13

A Grammy and the KKK

We always felt that since we were so unusual in our approach to gospel music that we should do unusual things. When Dottie sang solos she always put so much *soul* into her singing that she sounded as if she were black. I teased her from the stage, telling the audiences, "She's part Cherokee, and when you hear her sing you'll know what the other part is."

I suppose that comment was what gave me the idea of recording Dottie on a solo album using an all-black choir as backup. We looked around and chose twenty members of the Rev. Jonathon Greer's choir from Nashville.

Brother Greer didn't know us, nor did he know our music, so he delayed giving us an affirmative answer until he'd checked us out. "I loved that," Dottie said, "because I had checked on them, too."

The choir came to the RCA studios in Nashville and joined Dottie and they had a tremendous time doing the album. The preacher would come in and anoint everybody so they would sing in the Spirit. Dottie would be singing along and the director, a little black woman, would detect something wrong in the choir, and she'd stop the music and say, "Lord have mercy, that little

Cherokee Indian is blacker'n anybody here. You all stop right now and listen to what she's doing."

This was during the days in the sixties when Dr. Martin Luther King was marching, Alabama was rioting, and Mississippi was burning. When the album came out, titled *The Soul of Me*, and Dottie won the first Grammy ever given to a white singer for singing soul music, some folks were unhappy. That was the only Grammy we ever won but we were nominated eight or ten times. I don't remember how many Doves we won—those are the gospel music awards—but there were several.

When Dottie won that Grammy, Owen Bradley of Decca Records' Nashville office made us an offer he probably thought we couldn't refuse. He told us if we would sign a contract with Decca for Dottie to sing rhythm and blues, that Decca would put unlimited funds behind us.

This was the second major offer (remember Warner Bros.) we'd had to swing away from gospel, and we didn't immediately refuse it.

Dottie said to Bradley, "Let me think about it. We'll talk about it tomorrow."

Dottie and I talked it over that night and while we might have been tempted to accept, we turned it down. I'm sure we could have accepted the offer and remained good Christians, but we felt it wasn't what God had called us to do, and it wasn't what we wanted to do. We had no problem with turning the offer down.

We had really taken a chance putting that album out with the black choir. Bob McKenzie produced it and did a first-rate job, but the only thing that seemed to matter was that we had used a black backup choir. It ruffled a lot of feathers and we got all kinds of flak, lots of it. You'd be surprised if we told you how many letters we got from so-called Christians calling us "nigger-lovers."

But the crowning blow was the death threat we received from the Ku Klux Klan. We were scheduled to sing a concert in Jackson, Mississippi, and it had been advertised in *The Singing News* and other places. We got a letter from the KKK saying if we showed up for the concert, they would kill all of us.

On Sunday afternoon, we walked into the Jackson City Auditorium with an escort of four agents from the Federal Bureau of Investigation.

I told Dottie, "Now, Dottie, you be careful. Don't get us in trouble. Just play it cool."

I could tell that Dottie couldn't imagine anyone being upset over a group of Christian people, black or white, or black and white, getting up and singing about God. She has such a blind, staggering faith in God that she was near the boiling point. She reasoned this way: God gave me the gift and the ministry and He said He was going to take care of me. She was never frightened. Everybody else was sort of on pins and needles, but Dottie just went on as if nothing was happening.

Two thousand people filled the Jackson City Auditorium and tension ran high until Dottie got happy. When Dottie gets happy, she gets a Holy boldness. She started telling the audience about the death threats and she invited the KKK to come forward and let us pray for them. Once she opened up her arms and said, "Here I stand. If you want to shoot me for singing with twenty spiritual people who know God, here I am; go ahead and shoot." Talk about four nervous FBI agents. The audience responded with a standing ovation in praise to the Lord.

In our spiritual walk with God, this was a great milestone. I was reared a bigot, believing, talking, and acting like a typical southern boy. We had only two black families living in our town, and their children went to another city to school.

Bigots come in all forms. I was reared a religious bigot. The Baptists and Pentecostals didn't have anything to do with each other, and if you were a Catholic or a Jew, that was the worst possible thing. My rearing also instilled in me a bigotry against women, and certainly a bigotry against other races.

It's really sad, but in the church world today there are few racially integrated churches.

God has torn away that prejudice in our lives, not only the prejudice against race, but against religion, too. It's strange that Christians will give their missionary money to Africa, but don't want a black family living next door. We marvel at the accomplishments and dedication of the Catholics, but fail to recognize them as brothers and sisters in Christ.

There is no place for such as this in the Kingdom of God, and no one's life is pleasing to God if it contains any kind of prejudice, whether it be racial or religious. We are not to judge, and prejudice is judging our fellowman.

My growth from bigotry has been a gradual process. I suppose that day in Jackson was a part of it. In my Christian walk with God, I've met so many great Christian black people that I gradually grew out of my prejudice toward them. I suppose the biggest aid was our moving to Atlanta in the 1980s and joining Brother Earl Paulk's Chapel Hill Harvester Church. That's probably the most integrated church in America. Dr. Paulk marched with Martin Luther King and was a part of that whole movement.

To see Christians of all colors working in harmony is a tremendous thing, and we saw it constantly in that church. We participated, and we loved it.

I think we're doing a grave injustice in the church by having separation of the races. God can never really and truly bless a church until it reaches that point.

Perhaps the greatest force in removing racial prejudice from my life came in the form of a black woman named May Kate Collier. When we moved our house trailer to Nashville about the time Reba was twelve or thirteen years old, we decided we needed and could afford some periodic domestic help. We talked to our pastor and he recommended May Kate Collier, who worked part-time for him.

We got in touch with her and she agreed to help us one day a week, but it wasn't long, with our newfound success and affluence, that she was working full-time for us.

Through those difficult years, Katie helped raise Reba. Actually, you could probably say she also helped raise Dottie and me. We were just kids.

There was such a gentle, sweet, kind spirit in Katie. She could walk in the house and even if you didn't know she was there, you could almost feel her presence.

She worked for us about twenty years and I never noticed the fact that Katie was black. She was part of our family. Being around her changed my ideas of the black race a lot. If I ever met a Christian on this earth, I believe it was Katie.

CHAPTER 14

Not an Easy Task

Our struggle to get not necessarily to the top of the gospel singing world, but certainly to an elevated position, was not easy. It required years of scraping to make ends meet, of my working at other employment to earn an income, of scrimping and saving, and of utter disappointments both within and outside the church, because our first calling was and has always been to the church. Very simply, some would say, we had to pay our dues.

The concert world was a world all its own. Born out of singing schools that taught people to sing music with the solfeggio method—using shaped notes—it grew into a sizeable business in the years immediately following World War II.

But almost all the groups were male quartets, four men singing the parts—lead, first tenor, baritone, and bass—with a male piano player as accompanist. During those years the most popular groups were the Statesmen, the Blackwood Brothers, the Homeland Harmony Quartet, the Stamps Quartet, the Blue Ridge Quartet, the Harvesters, the Rangers, the Harmoneers, all of whom were all-male groups. On one hand you could count the major groups that had female vocalists—the Chuck Wagon Gang, the LeFevres, sometimes the Happy Goodman Family, and the Speer Family. There were others in both categories, of course, but those are the ones that first come to mind.

Suddenly, here came the Rambos! Three people singing, and two were women. Our instruments were an accordion, two guitars, and a bass. No piano. In the world of gospel music, we must have been strange and certainly unconventional. Groups often stood off and laughed at us.

We didn't even sing the same part in every song; we sang an inverted harmony, something that few groups tried to do then but many make the most of today. We weren't being smart; we inverted the harmony out of necessity. I would sing lead until it became too high for me, then Reba would take over the lead and I would drop to tenor or alto, and then we would change keys and Dottie would sing the lead. We found this easier for us than the conventional method of singing harmony.

There is a harmony in family voices that no amount of practice can achieve. Reba's piercing high gave us a unique blend and everyone loved her.

Eventually, though, those in the business came to realize that no one liked our style "but the people." That became our slogan. And then it was our turn to laugh—but never openly—when other groups began scrambling to find guitar and bass players.

Dottie's songwriting became such a force in gospel music that on several occasions she had four songs in the top ten of the charts. When other groups began to sing her songs, I suppose we were then fully accepted by the gospel singing fraternity.

Many who have been singing gospel all their lives have said that the Rambos were responsible for the biggest change in gospel music ever. The popularity and the heights we attained encouraged so many other family groups to come into the field that it was said we revolutionized gospel music, turning the emphasis from the male quartets to family groups.

It has also been said that we were chiefly responsible for switching gospel music from strictly an entertainment to a heartfelt ministry in which thousands of people have given their hearts and souls to Jesus and completely changed their lives.

If we did this, I am proud of it. Although many of those in the field of gospel music sing for such great ministries as Billy Graham, gospel music had not then become the soul-winning endeavor that it has now achieved.

Most gospel groups today consider themselves to be in a ministry—a change brought only in recent years. The Rambos always felt that way about our work.

But we wanted to make good music—our kind of music. When we came on the scene, those who were making it were doing so with four voices and a piano. Heaven forbid when we started dragging out drums, steel guitars and accordions.

People said, "You can't do that!" But we did.

A lot of times, Dottie and I played guitars, Reba played the bass, and Pat played the accordion. We were told that we couldn't make it that way. Three-part harmony? We were told we'd have trouble making it that way, also. Seemingly, every time we turned around, we went against the grain.

They also told us that we couldn't get by singing all-original songs, that we had to sing the old standbys. But they failed to consider the power of Dottie Rambo's songs.

We had all these strikes against us, but we didn't know it. We just did what we could do and people liked it.

It took us a long time to realize that Dottie's songs were affecting people's lives. They still do. When you begin to realize that the songs you do on stage have an affect on people's lives, then you're no longer singing for the moment—you're singing for eternity. That can be an overwhelming thought. There was a strength and a power in Dottie's songs and in that three-chord strand—the Rambos singing together.

We were competitive with other groups, yes. We tried to make them really have to work just to be able to sing on the same stage with us. But through all the competition, there was still the thought that we wanted to sing something that would touch people, not just put a high ending on a song, or to get an exceptional blend of voices regardless of what we were singing, but to sing something that really mattered.

Reba put it this way: "We never wanted to sing Pablum, songs that simply had good arrangements just so we could sound good on stage. Yes, we wanted to have fun, but what we did sing—had to have values."

Reba knows music, and she had Dottie and me summed up pretty well, especially in our talents. She gauged Dottie by the strength of her songs, which put her on the top rung of Reba's admiration ladder. She said I was harder to teach, but once I learned a song, I remembered it, and I do. I could sing those songs right now that we did twenty years ago. "We would dig up one of our old songs," Reba said, "that some of us had forgotten parts of, and Dad would say, 'Now, this is the way the part went,' and would sing it without missing a note. He is our memory bank. He stores everything well."

We didn't rise to the top of the gospel concert world by default or accident, nor in any other way than hard work—and when we got there, the spotlight almost destroyed us.

CHAPTER 15

Prosperity Street

We finally turned the corner onto Prosperity Street—and it almost wrecked our lives.

Gospel concerts were big business in all the major cities of the South, and in many of the smaller ones, too. People hungered for gospel music. We were in demand all over, and we sang five or six concerts a week.

Money came in like it was manna from Heaven, and I suppose I viewed it as such for a while. We were just like most other people who never had anything and suddenly struck it rich.

We bought a huge antebellum home, the kind with a cement pond. Transportation had always been our problem, but it wasn't any more. I bought Dottie a new Cadillac Fleetwood and myself an Eldorado and paid cash for both.

Recognition came our way. People recognized us on the streets. We sang on the Grand Ole Opry. Our first appearance on the Opry was a bit unusual. It was not by prearrangement; it was a spur-of-the-moment thing.

We went to the Opry one night to enjoy ourselves. They hadn't built Opryland yet, and the Opry was still presented in Ryman Auditorium. A number of country music stars were among our friends and acquaintances and during the program Dottie, Reba, and I went backstage to shake some hands and say hello to some of the performers. Grant Turner, the Opry announcer, came over to us and asked, "Would you all sing for us?"

That surprised me. We had no idea anyone connected with the Opry even knew who we were. But it also pleased me. "Well," I said, "yeah, but we'll have to go get our guitars."

We had not gone to the Opry prepared to sing, but there are some things you'll do without preparation, and singing on the Opry was one of them. We got a flat-top guitar and a piano and someone found a snare drum, and we got some of the Opry's musicians who had played recording sessions for us, and we were ready.

Turner announced us and we walked out there scared to death and sang "The Holy Hills of Heaven Call Me" and followed that with "He Looked Beyond My Faults and Saw My Need," and tore up the house. The audience responded so well to our music that we were never again frightened to go on the Opry.

When we lived in Nashville before we moved to California, we'd just walk in to the Opry and they'd ask us to sing. We sang several times there, sometimes by prearrangement, often by impromptu invitation. It was always strange to us that these country fans applauded when we were introduced just like we were at a gospel concert. I think the majority of people who love gospel music also love country. I know I do. Country music and gospel are really kissing cousins. When you sing gospel or country, you're addressing people's emotions.

One thing about singing on the Opry that was always frustrating to us was the Opry's lack of stage monitors. Gospel people were accustomed to having real hot monitors throwing the sound back at them, but the Grand Ole Opry at that time used no monitors. You were supposed to sing with musical instruments only. When we sang there without monitors, it was strange because we felt nobody was hearing us.

Not long after our first appearance, Opryland was built and the Grand Ole Opry moved there.

We were familiar with Ryman long before we went on the

Opry. We used to attend Wally Fowler's All-Night Sings there and then we sang on them several times, and we also sang on the Gospel Opry at Ryman.

On the road, we had great fun, not only in singing but in our everyday lives.

Once we were scheduled to work a Fair, which had been hit hard by rain for several days. The stage area was flooded and the Fair people had set up a provisional stage on a flatbed truck out in a nearby field. They ran a strip of lights over the stage, and when we began to sing those lights began to attract grasshoppers. The field must have contained a million grasshoppers.

Reba has a deathly fear of three things: snakes, spiders, and, for some strange reason, grasshoppers. She can't stand them.

She was almost in tears when we reached the stage, but I told her, "Now, Reba, calm yourself. You know the rules: if you can walk, you can go; and if you can talk, you can sing—grasshoppers or not."

Bravely Reba sang. I would look at Reba and she would be looking at her mother—and Dottie had grasshoppers in her hair and crawling over her back, and every time Reba looked at her she shuddered. Reba had worn a wig on stage that night, and when we finished singing she made a mad dash for the bus, ripping off the wig and shaking the grasshoppers out as she ran. She dove on the bus and charged into her room and slammed the door. Charlie Black, our bus driver, was standing conveniently by, and when Reba plunged into her room, Charlie locked her in. He and some of the guys in the band had spent an hour or two catching grasshoppers and had put a few hundred of them in Reba's room!

They stood around in the bus laughing and slapping their legs, listening to her cry and scream in the little cubicle, and after about five minutes they let her out. She looked as if she'd just gone through an Alfred Hitchcock scene.

Once at the National Quartet Convention, I wanted all of us to look exceptionally sharp, so I bought new white outfits for everyone. The girls had new white dresses, and I thought we would look spectacular on stage.

I told everybody I would buy the suits but each had to furnish his own white shoes. All the guys except Kenny Hicks bought new white shoes. Kenny, our bass player who later became personal valet to Elvis, decided to save his money. He bought a can of white spray paint and painted his black patent-leather shoes.

Kenny was a big old heavy guy who was a comedian. I knew I'd better check with him and make sure he had conformed.

"Kenny," I asked the day of our convention appearance, "you've got your white shoes, haven't you?"

"Gotcha covered," Kenny replied, giving me a thumbs up.

He put on his painted shoes and walked out on stage, and the paint had dried and was cracking and peeling off, and I felt like turning him over my knee. He just grinned and kept picking.

We had a box of old combination locks in the luggage bay of the bus, and I picked out two of them that were open, whose combinations had long since been lost and forgotten, and ran them through the buckles on Kenny's painted shoes and locked them. When he discovered he couldn't get the locks unlocked, he had to throw the shoes away and buy a new pair anyway.

Judy Sproles was one of Reba's closest friends. The daughter of a pastor, Judy came to live with us in Nashville and she and Reba grew even closer.

She and Reba were both about seventeen, and she traveled with us and sang with Reba in the group we called Charity's Children. I paid them salaries and gave each a food allowance on the road.

They saved their money and bought two designer suede coats. Reba's was blue with butterflies on the back, and Judy's was earthtones with a sunset scene. To buy the coats, the girls had not only saved all they could, but had begged and borrowed every penny they could from others in our group. They even came to me and collected a week's pay in advance. I told them, "That's fine, but don't come to me for more money. If you're going to buy those stupid coats, that's it!" I was trying to teach them some responsibility in handling money.

They spent every dime they had, including all their food money, for the coats.

The first day wasn't too bad. We had some fruit baskets on the bus and they crammed themselves with fruit. After the concert that night, we stopped at a truck stop and I told them, "I don't want to see you begging money from anybody," and all they had was coffee.

The next day they were famished. When we sang a concert that evening, two brothers—whom the girls didn't really care for—showed up. They were homely as sin, and we thought it was funny the way the girls decided to talk to them that evening, each time maneuvering them close to the concession stand, and then one of the girls would say, "Oh, those tacos look great, don't they?"

And one of the boys would answer, "Would you like some?" I thought the girls were going to shove whole tacos in their mouths.

When the concert ended, I overheard Reba say to the boys, "Would you guys like to go eat?"

Judy said, "Boy, I'd just love a steak."

"Let's go," said the boys.

They ate two steaks each with all the trimmings.

That was a week in which Reba and Judy learned how to fend for themselves—and how to con their friends.

We were truly successful in a material way, but it wasn't long until an ugly head reared before us. I don't mean to knock anyone's prosperity doctrine, but just because you're prosperous does not mean it's a Godly prosperity. We were singing the best we ever had, drawing big crowds everywhere; we were in the charts, and Dottie was writing her best songs. We were making money hand over fist—and for many people, that would have been Utopia.

Our annual income at the height of our career would be difficult to say. We had gotten to the place that we were well into the six-figure bracket, $100,000 plus. We were making lots of money, but lots of money then wouldn't be much money today.

But we had been called and anointed to sing and preach the Gospel, and we had become so busy making money and entertaining people that we forgot about His Church and His cause.

I personally believe it is easier to live for God in times of struggle, and if you aren't careful, very careful, prosperity will kill you.

With us, it became an obsession to outdo any group that walked on stage. We sang harder, trying to draw louder applause and standing ovations than anyone else. Most Christians do not know the difference between anointed singing and show biz, to become the biggest name, to sell more records, to draw the biggest crowds—and it almost destroyed us.

Dottie and I became business partners instead of husband and wife, and it almost caused us to divorce. My spiritual man was falling apart and then my physical man followed. I became very ill. I was hospitalized five times in 1970 with heart trouble. My heart stopped during my last heart attack and I had an out-of-body experience. Everyone thought I was dead. The doctors eventually got my heart started and that event changed my life.

I was in the Intensive Care Unit of Nashville Memorial Hospital. Dottie, J.D. Sumner, and David Ludwyck, my lawyer, were sitting outside ICU, waiting to see me. I didn't know they were there.

Suddenly, I just left my body. I started floating outside the room and down the hall and I looked down and saw Dottie, J.D., and David sitting there talking quietly. That was probably the only time in my life I had total peace, a total absence of fear and frustration. It was absolutely the most gorgeous peace I have ever known. I was floating toward a light and was almost at the end of the hall when suddenly I realized I was back in my body.

I said, "I don't want to go back." Whatever was happening was so great. I can't begin to explain the feeling, the total absence of fear, anxiety, everything but peace. An emergency team had shocked me back to life; they were all around me, working feverishly, and whatever they did—worked.

But I told my family later that if that ever happens again—
don't bring me back. Let me go.

I have had no fear of death since then.

CHAPTER 16

Rambos in Vietnam

There really was a Rambo in Vietnam.

Three of them, in fact. Dottie and I and our daughter, Reba, were there. We carried no automatic weapons, nor any grenades. Our weapons were guitars and voices that sang songs of inspiration to the troops who fought a sometimes invisible enemy in the lush, green jungles of this faraway Asian land. We were accustomed to fighting an invisible enemy; we've been doing that all our lives.

Although we took no active part in combat, we were shot at, and our helicopter sustained hits from Vietcong ground fire. It shuddered but carried us safely if somewhat shaken to our destination.

That was in 1967 when the Vietnam War was at its height. We had been singing the Gospel for a number of years and were probably at a peak of popularity as gospel singers go in the United States. A friend of ours, Ken Duncan, a gospel music promoter in Southern Illinois, Missouri, and Indiana, contacted us about making a tour of Vietnam to sing for the military forces. There were yards of red tape to cut, especially that concerning Reba, who was only fifteen years old; but finally we agreed to a six-weeks tour that would carry us into the combat zones to entertain the front-line troops and we were cleared by the State Department to make the tour.

That clearance was easy to come by because we had already paved the way. A year earlier, in 1966, we had made a six-week tour of our northern outposts in Greenland, and of Newfoundland, Labrador, and Iceland, and the State Department received great and pleasing response to that tour.

Actually, it was a piece of cake, entertaining the troops in those northern areas. Talk about a desolate place—and entertainment-starved troops!

The first place we went to was the Strategic Air Command base in Thule, Greenland, where all those B-52 bombers sat on the ready line, loaded with bombs for retaliation in case the Soviet Union attacked us in the Cold War.

The troops assigned to Thule were sent there for a whole year, and the isolation and solitude was enough to drive some crazy. We were told numerous suicides occurred among our troops there.

We sang to small numbers of people, lived with them, and went to the movies with them. There were only eight women in Thule—military nurses—and Dottie lived with them. I lived with the troops. Every time we performed, it was like playing to homefolks.

So when Ken Duncan approached the State Department about sending entertainment to Vietnam, someone in the State Department remembered our adventure in Thule and suggested, "The Rambos did such a great job at Thule, why don't we send them to Vietnam?"

Next thing we knew, we were on the way.

Gospel singers often are accused of singing only for money, but that isn't the case—certainly not all the time, anyway. We—the Singing Rambos—always tried to minister through song whether we were paid for what we did or not. And through the years we've done a lot of mission work for which we did not expect to receive pay. Greenland and Vietnam were part of that mission work.

Our pay for the Vietnam venture was negligible. For the six weeks, the government agreed to pay us each—Dottie, Reba, Pat Jones, and me—eight dollars a day. Out of this, we would each pay three dollars daily for lodging, and use the other five dollars to purchase food. Our transportation would be provided via military aircraft, both to and from Vietnam and while we were there.

Obviously, we would need financial assistance for such a venture, and I contacted some of our church friends, those to whom we had been singing to for years, and asked for financial aid in this undertaking. After all, how often does a gospel group get to visit and minister in a war zone? This was to be a special trip in which many people could take part simply by sharing the burden with us.

So I wrote to two hundred churches, asking for financial help. Three churches responded with a total of $350. I didn't see how we could survive, but we were already committed and cleared, so we went on anyway.

In February 1967 we departed Andrews Air Force Base bound for Vietnam. The flight lasted twenty-two hours, stopping in Honolulu, Guam, and finally Saigon.

As we approached Saigon, the beautiful jungle terrain of Vietnam spread out below us. We were periodically briefed on things we could expect, and as we made the landing approach, we were told that we would come in for a spiral landing, maintaining a safe altitude until our Boeing 707 was over the landing site, then in quick circles we would descend to the landing field. This was to keep us beyond range of Vietcong gunfire. The airfield and its perimeter were cleared of enemy troops during the day, but they filtered back in to firing range at night.

Our hearts were in our throats as the captain eased back on the throttles and the four powerful jet engines changed pitch and lost power, and the aircraft began to descend in circles, losing about a thousand feet each time it circled. No one from the ground fired a shot at us as we finally straightened out and slipped quickly and carefully onto the landing strip. Believe me, the captain of that plane knew how to control his craft.

We had been on the ground only a few minutes when I was informed that all of my luggage had been stolen and nothing could be done about it. The Vietnamese black market even reached into the luggage bays at the airfield.

To make matters worse, we were told we must leave the air base quickly for the thirty-mile drive into Saigon. "Hurry, hurry!" our adviser pushed us. "It is almost dark, and the Vietcong control the highway after dark!"

That put us in a rush. Not wishing to be shot at from such a close range, we gathered up such of our belongings as were left— including Dottie, Pat, and Reba's suitcases—and piled into a jeep. The driver, a sergeant, meshed the gears and we rolled through the gates of the air base onto the open road, and there he put the pedal to the metal and drove the thirty miles to the city at breakneck speed. We felt we were on a roller coaster, sailing along that road which was lined with rice paddies, from the air base to Saigon.

Winding through the teeming streets of Saigon, we soon came to the military hotel in which we would be quartered, and the driver whipped the jeep into the parking decks inside the hotel, wiped his brow, grinned, and said, "Wow! We made it!"

The four of us agreed with his sentiments exactly.

That evening I wore the clothing I had worn since we left the states, and in mid-morning of the day following our arrival, a soldier drove me to the military post exchange, the PX, to buy some clothes to wear. I thought about the type of things I would buy and decided on simple things in which I would be comfortable in the jungle's oppressive heat. But when we arrived and walked into the PX, the sights I saw were enough to make a common man fighting mad.

The PX had nothing to sell. Long rows of shelves, which should have been stocked with all sorts of things, were almost bare. The store was nearly empty. There were plenty of clerks but they had nothing to sell!

Yet, outside, the sidewalks were lined with Vietnamese selling American-made clothing, mostly G.I. garb, pots and pans, trinkets of all sorts, electronic things; you name it, they had it. Everything you would expect to find in the PX was on sale at exorbitantly inflated black market rates on the sidewalks around the PX.

I refused to be part of such a thing; I refused to purchase my wearing apparel on the black market, and finally a young soldier, who was my size, loaned me some army fatigues, and this was what I wore for the entire six weeks in Vietnam.

When we went to the supply area to receive the sound equipment for our concerts, the civilian personnel wouldn't help us. They were employees of the Armed Forces Entertainment Unit, hired to handle all the professional entertainment for the military, but they ignored us as completely as if we'd been in New York City. After several attempts to get help, we gave up and went to the warehouse, found what we needed, put it together, and eventually got ourselves ready to go to work. That was probably in our favor, because the equipment I chose and put together was so compact it fit easily into a helicopter with room enough left over for the four of us and our military escort, an army captain who stayed with us from the time we touched down at that airfield until we lifted off again on our way home.

Our experiences in Vietnam convinced me that we did not lose that war because of our military. It was because of the noncaring U.S. civilian population and the miles and miles of red tape of the bureaucracy that made it impossible for our troops to fight a war. Had we not been accustomed to making our way around uncaring personnel, we would have missed half of our concerts.

Carefully, we fixed all of our sound equipment and instruments so they would fit in the limited space inside a helicopter, which gave us the mobility we needed to hit the ground, get things set up, and be in concert within thirty minutes. When we realized we could achieve such mobility with the help of military personnel, we decided to do three or four concerts a day, depending on how much time we would have to be in the air going from place to place.

It is impossible to explain Vietnam to people who were not there. What a terrible place to have to fight a war! The foliage was so thick, our military often had to cut its way through. The Vietcong were masters at boobytrapping, and many of our young men died in their traps. There were no front lines as such, only fighting areas, and an area cleared today of Vietcong would be overrun by them again tonight.

It was not an easy place to do concerts, either. Rain fell all the time we were there. Most of our concerts were done off the back of a truck for a stage. The men who came to hear us sing would sit right down in the mud.

We designed our concerts to last for an hour, but because of the tremendous response of our troops, most went for two hours. They were the hungriest people for entertainment that we had ever faced.

Dottie, Reba, and Pat Jones, our accordionist, decided they would wear the same kind of clothes they sang in back home. They wore combat boots to the stage, then put on high heels—and the boys loved it.

We were never advertised as gospel singers; we were just entertainment and they usually introduced us incorrectly as "The Swinging Rambos." Those in charge of our tour didn't know how gospel would be received; so we started our programs with Dottie playing "Wildwood Flower" on the guitar. Then we sang a song about home, then one about Mama, and then one about Jesus. By that time, the guys would accept anything we sang or said. To say that the Vietnam audiences gave us our greatest experiences as singers and musicians sounds trivial, but this was definitely the highlight of our singing careers.

We covered as much ground as we could in the six weeks. We sang in the Delta to the Green Berets. We sang to the Cobra and Lancer helicopter squadrons, who were definitely the unsung heroes of Vietnam. In the Demilitarized Zone, the DMZ, we sang to General Ryan's troops, and we sang in isolated areas where the troops had not seen any live entertainment in thirteen months. We sang to every unit we could get to.

After many concerts, they gave us captured Vietcong flags and made us honorary members of their units. These are memories not too many entertainers ever get to accumulate.

Like the troops, we slept in tents, ate C-rations packed in 1949, and Dottie, who isn't a big girl to begin with, lost fifteen pounds the six weeks we were there, mostly on account of the diet. The girls had a great deal of difficulty with their appearance. Because of the monsoons, when anything got wet, we couldn't get it dry again. Eventually our shoes molded. The girls dared not wash their long hair; so they just sprayed it with more hair spray and went their merry ways.

Few who went to the combat areas failed to experience the hazards of war. Once, after a late-afternoon concert, we were trying to get our plane packed and get off the runway before dark when the Vietcong began throwing mortar shells into the air base. Jumping in the plane, we took off and watched from the air as the Vietcong attacked the base.

Another time, we flew low over the jungle and our chopper was hit by enemy rifle fire from the ground.

In one area, an outdoor arena had been built for the Bob Hope Christmas Show, and the fighting had been so bad they had cancelled the show and moved it to a safer location. We were asked if we would go there and do the concert, and we readily accepted the invitation.

When our helicopter arrived and we were ushered to the arena, our mouths fell open in surprise. As far as we could see, there were thousands of servicemen and women, many on cots and stretchers.

For a brief time, the rain stopped, and we began our concert in warm sunshine. Eventually that show became something of a camp meeting. It ended with us off the platform, walking among the troops, ministering to them, looking at photos of their kids, and having a great time.

We visited field hospitals and sang to the wounded. We prayed for and held the hands of the dying. These were heartbreaking experiences; they were like no other times we had ever known.

One of the things we noticed most was the youthfulness of our fighting men in Vietnam. I suppose it struck Reba the hardest blow. She was only fifteen, and she felt that most of the G.I.'s we saw were guys she could have dated. "You didn't see Playboy Magazines," she said, "you saw comic books."

Once, at the end of a performance, before we left the stage, I suggested, "Let's go out and meet these boys and talk to them." An officer overheard and said, "You can't do that! There's no telling what they'd say." While I engaged the officer in conversation, Dottie, Reba, and Pat made their way through a portion of the audience, and in a few moments I joined them. The troops treated us with the utmost respect. Some showed us pictures of their moms, and others showed pictures of their wives or girlfriends. We were a family and we were safe to them, and they felt that I had taken a great risk bringing my family over there. There weren't that many family shows that hit Vietnam. I don't know how many others; maybe none.

Our experiences there were strange to us. One night we were trapped in a forward area and had to spend the night where we hadn't been scheduled. This place was too dangerous for us to stay because the VC lobbed mortars into the area every night, but the chopper that was supposed to take us out got called to another mission and couldn't make it back for us.

We were in the DMZ and were guests of General Ryan. They gave me accommodations in an officer's tent, and Dottie, Reba, and Pat were put in an old tin-roofed shed. General Ryan very graciously permitted them to use his personal outhouse. Instead of a crescent moon, it had a star in the door, and from that star someone had hung a crude sign that read, "Ladies Only."

Rain poured all night and sometime during the night, Reba had to go to the outhouse. Her stomach was upset from the food and she had to go in the worst way. Occasional mortar shells dropped into the base, but not any had come close to the area where we stayed.

Reba put on her fatigues, a big coat, camouflage hat, and combat boots and ran the fifty yards through mud to the general's outhouse, literally leaping bunkers in the rain.

When she finished her task in the outhouse, she buttoned up, opened the door, and stepped out—and five G.I.'s were standing there with rifles on the outhouse and fingers on the triggers. They had seen a person they didn't know running to the outhouse, and thought it might have been a VC who had sneaked into the base.

Reba saw the guns and screamed and fainted, and the guys, realizing who she was, grabbed her up and carried her quickly through the rain back to the shack in which she was sleeping.

The helicopters we rode in were shot at constantly, and sometimes ground fire scored hits on our aircraft. The sides of the choppers were usually open so the gunners could maneuver their weapons to fire back at the VC, and in flight the gunners sat with legs dangling over the sides. We didn't worry so much about being hit ourselves, but worried about those gunners getting hit in their legs.

We were almost in a surrealistic state of mind. We didn't really worry about being shot. I don't believe any of us thought we might be killed. A feeling akin to invincibility came over us after a few days in Vietnam.

The girls saw sights that would turn ordinary stomachs. We visited field hospitals and walked among the dying. One young man was so burned, his hands and face were black; and there seemed to be so few people to help in those hospital units. Once Dottie and Reba helped dress wounds, and Reba even gave a guy a shot to calm him until he could be lifted out by helicopter.

In a driving rain, we went into a hospital tent. One end of the tent was soggy and somewhat open, and stretcher cases lay there awaiting surgery. The surgical unit was in the other end of the tent where it was dry. Three young men lay waiting for the surgeons, and one's body was so ripped and torn we couldn't tell which end was which.

An orderly said, "He's not going to make it." Dottie and Reba went to him and he opened one eye and looked at them and asked in a faint voice, "Are you angels?" Dottie began to pray with him and he died while she held his hand, but when he went his eyes were smiling.

Then, aboard fixed-wing aircraft, we flew out to the Seventh Fleet in the South China Sea and landed first on the aircraft carrier *Ticonderoga*. From the air, the flight deck looked like a postage stamp, but our pilot put us on the deck with apparent ease. Of course, not any of us had ever landed on an aircraft carrier, and when the pilot put the plane down and we hit the deck, a hook in the tail of the plane grabbed a cable and jerked us to a halt. You can't imagine how quickly you can stop on the deck of an aircraft carrier!

After four concerts aboard the *Ticonderoga*, we flew to the aircraft carrier *Kitty Hawk*. There we sang to 5,000 men just before they launched the biggest air strike of the war against Hanoi. We were taken to the ready room to pray with the outgoing pilots. Eight of these men did not return.

"The ministry we did in Vietnam was the most wonderful thing I did in my life," Dottie said. She remembers talking to a red-headed young pilot on the *Ticonderoga* prior to a mission to bomb Hanoi.

Just before he went out to board his plane, he turned to Dottie and asked, "Would you mind praying with me?"

"Sure, Red," she replied and took his hand. After the prayer she asked, "How is your relationship with the Lord? Do you know Him?"

"Yes, ma'am," Red said. "Everything's fine."

"Then go right on," Dottie said. "God knows what He's doing, and no matter what happens, it's all in God's plan."

Red didn't come back.

We were given commendations both by Gen. William Westmoreland, the supreme commander in Vietnam, and by the admiral of the Seventh Fleet, but no award could ever erase the memory of the thousands of men and women we ministered to.

In Vietnam, we sang the last song many a soul heard.

I'm so glad it was a song about Jesus!

CHAPTER 17

New Commitments

Dottie and I finally sat down and made some new commitments. We agreed that if God would heal my body, heal our marriage, and once again place His anointing on us, that we would never again walk on a stage and put on a show for anyone.

We would put our ministry back in the church where it belonged and our lives would be spent in His service.

Don't take this as a put-down of good people who perform in gospel concerts in auditoriums. God can walk those aisles as surely as He walks through the church. There is nothing wrong with good, clean entertainment, even in gospel concerts. Gospel singing is filled with strong people who can handle this. To be sure, there are some ministers who would have more appeal if they would let down their religious fronts and just laugh once in a while with the congregation. We enjoyed the entertainment aspects of other groups, and some were really funny.

When we came on the concert scene, most of concert gospel music was entertainment. There were a few old war-horses who blessed your socks, people like Mom and Dad Speer, Vestal and Howard Goodman, and Eva Mae Lefevre. But, remember, we were fresh out of the local churches, revival fires were burning

128

in us, and to be perfectly honest, we were not about to put out the flames.

Promoters booked some groups because of their great singing, like the Blackwood Brothers; and booked others, like the Lewis Family, because of their great music. And some promoters booked us because we added a spiritual impact to the concerts. I don't know exactly how we made it; probably we were pretty good singers. Dottie was unique playing the guitar. But I feel that when we sang, we were always anointed by the Holy Spirit, and we allowed that spirit to move when we sang. We didn't go into comedy but sang as the spirit led us to sing.

Normally this made it hard for a group to follow us in concert; unless, of course, the group could sing under that same anointing. So, most groups asked the promoters not to schedule them to follow us, but to be on before we sang. Looking back, I can see where we used that anointing to our own advantage, and we did many groups an injustice by our attitude, which was simply, "we'll just blow the walls down and see if you can follow it."

Before you judge us too quickly, I've seen the same thing done in Bible conferences and in pulpits all across America by preachers trying to out-preach other preachers. This is called "show business" and may God deliver us from it even today.

Some of the greatest people I know sing the Gospel, and some of my fondest memories are when groups could lay aside their planned programs and join together on stage and just enjoy the presence of God. It's too bad that some people had to live sixty years before they realized that God was at work even then, despite our ability to realize it. It was God who lifted us up from kids singing in street meetings to grown-ups singing in huge buildings filled with thousands of Gospel-hungry, needy people.

I read an article in a gospel music magazine recently that listed people who had made the greatest impact of anyone on gospel music. Names like Mom and Dad Speer, James Blackwood, the Goodmans, even Bill Gaither were not even mentioned. Shame on an industry that forgets the giants who blazed the trail so that others may coast through life. The names the writer mentioned included some I had never heard of. One thing we do know is that God keeps good records, and He knows.

Some day we will all stand before God and be judged according to our works. The Bible speaks of a new song. I believe many of the people we have worked with for a lifetime will be there. All our physical labor will be ended and for eternity we will join together and sing "Worthy Is the Lamb." We will cast our crowns at His feet and Vestal and Dottie will join with George Younce and others to sing, and maybe even I could join in. Now that will be a concert worth hearing.

I learned much from the veterans of gospel music. They seemed to enjoy teaching the tricks of the trade to others like me. The first time we ever sang with the Lefevres, when the concert was over I went out on stage to help put away the P.A. system, and I started wadding up the microphone cords. Pierce Lefevre came to me and kindly said, "Buck, let me show you how to roll up the cords correctly, and then you'll always know." I never forgot that lesson, and until this day I have never rolled up a cord except the correct way. Ben Speer taught me more about sound systems than anyone. I learned to be professional, which really means to be responsible.

I learned from the greatest. No one likes a know-it-all; they usually don't last long in the kingdom, and everyone can teach you something. With this always in mind, I listened and learned. I learned about how concerts are promoted from W.B. Nowlin, J.G. Whitfield, Sonny Simmons, Lloyd Orrell, and others. From the Prophets Quartet and Speer Family I learned to respond to other groups when their buses break down. They saved our hides more than once.

John T. Benson, Bob Benson, Bob McKenzie, and countless others taught me the publishing and recording businesses.

In case I ever forget to say thanks to them, I say it here. Thank you! Thank you! We are grateful for friends who showed us how and helped us make it. Like Rex Nelon and Wendy Bagwell who showed me how to have buddies on the road. From the Blackwood Brothers I learned how to travel across Canada in a crippled bus and how to rewire a bus on the move. We sang by night and traveled by day, and some of the Blackwoods traveled with us, rewiring as we went along.

I learned a great truth I would like to pass on to singers and preachers: No one likes to hear you sing for as much time as you want to sing. No one wants to hear you preach for the length of time you want to preach. Perhaps that sounds weird, but sometimes we go on so long that we abuse our audiences. No one likes to feel we are infringing on his time. My best advice is these two words: Condense it! Audiences bless you with their presence. Don't abuse them. Never feel that you are their source of blessing. They are our source of blessing. They buy our buses and homes, educate our children, and support us in every conceivable way. We are fortunate and blessed to even stand in a place of ministry. Always let the audience and God know how grateful you are for this grand and glorious privilege. God calls this being a servant.

Never criticize other forms of music or ministry. God can use any vehicle, whether it is rock, contemporary, country, or Southern style of gospel music. It may not be your cup of tea, but remember that God hasn't asked you to drink it. Even if it's a half-naked savage beating on a drum who just found Christ, making melody in his heart and loving Jesus, who are we to judge the package as long as Christ is exalted?

There are several nationally-known ministers I personally can't stand to hear, but who am I to judge? God uses people whom I would never call, but they reach a segment of humanity that might never enjoy our ministry.

To get back on subject, we found before too many years elapsed that we were not strong enough to work the concert circuit, outside the covering of the church.

Even though the church failed us, as it often will fail you because it is made up of imperfect people, it is still the structure that God has ordained, and we must have that association to be strong. The church is a haven for us.

The period that I was ill was not a good time for Reba. I had sold the bus and stopped traveling, and as Dottie and I had our problems, Reba became torn between us, the two people who loved her most. We caused her to make decisions that perhaps she would not have made if our lives had not been in such conflict.

I don't intend to tell Reba's story. Some day, this will be a major undertaking in her life, but I will hit the high spots here.

In the mid-1970s, she decided to marry a young man we had known all his life, Landy Gardner, the son of a Pentecostal preacher from Huntington, West Virginia. We had worked revivals in his church and Landy and Reba knew each other from childhood. Landy was a good young man—truly a wonderful person. Unfortunately, two of the greatest people in the world can't always make a marriage work and after four years they tearfully divorced. He is now choir director in the largest Pentecostal church in Nashville.

After Reba's marriage to Landy, she decided to quit singing with the family and try to make it on her own. To say I was crushed would be an understatement. When she told us she was leaving the family group, I went to bed and stayed for weeks. I just didn't care to get up. It hurt to think that Reba no longer wanted to sing or travel with us.

But she was right: There was no future for her at that time with Dottie and me. She cut a couple of solo records and was really doing well until her own marriage fell apart.

Reba traveled and sang for a year with Andre Crouch and the Disciples, and while it was a tough year, it was educational and rewarding for her. She was the only white girl in this black group, although there were a couple of white, male musicians.

Andre had bought my bus, and at least Reba felt somewhat at home in it. There were about twelve people packed into the bus, and it was the first time Reba had ever been in a multiracial, multicultural situation. Andre coached her in her singing until she melted right into the group, and she discovered there were parts of her voice that were untapped. She became a fuller and better singer during that year.

During this time of turmoil, a young girl named Patty Carpenter came with us. Patty didn't look like Reba, nor did she sound like Reba, but she was the kind of person everyone loved, and singing with us, she sounded great.

Reba loved her and helped her learn our songs, and things actually began looking better for us. I bought a new bus, hired a six-piece band, and announced we were going back to singing, not in concert halls but in churches.

Soon we realized how big the financial hole was that we were digging. It was a great change to leave the concert halls and the thousands of dollars they brought in; but I was determined to just sing in churches. I had thirteen people on the payroll and we worked churches for offerings of $200 a night when it cost me $2,000 to be there.

Through the first year, I went in the hole $250,000. We traveled and sang just as we had in the concert world, but the churches could not support us. I had trouble figuring it out. I was sure that as soon as they understood the sacrifices we were making for them, they would rally around and pull us out of the hole we were digging for ourselves.

Alas, no one did!

But God's work progressed. It is true that God works in mysterious ways, and I learned this many times through experience. During this time God was teaching me a great lesson.

A South Carolina promoter invited us to a concert and told me he would have a new building seating 5,000, and I thought I might recoup some losses there. He said if we would come, he would guarantee a full house. His words sounded great. What an opportunity!

On a hot Sunday afternoon, we arrived in South Carolina and found no building seating 5,000. Instead we found a metal building housing a horse show arena, and in the center of the riding ring were about 400 seats. When we turned on the P.A. system, the sound echoed off those metal walls like the Grand Canyon. But the house was full. Four hundred people showed up.

I don't like anyone to lie to me, and I was thoroughly disgusted that afternoon. The building was so hot we could barely stand it, and when we went on stage I was thinking, "Let's get this over with."

At the end of the program, I gave the usual invitation. In my heart I felt no one would respond, but I had promised God I would do this; so I asked, "If there is anyone here who does not know Jesus would you raise your hand."

When I saw two hundred hands go up, I was shocked. I said, "If you really mean this, then come forward for prayer."

The two hundred hungry souls rose from their seats and made their way toward the stage, and as they approached, God said to me, "They are coming not because of what you did here today but because My Holy Spirit is here. I do not need you. I can work even when you're angry. If you are going to do a work for Me, remember this: It's My spirit that draws men to repentence."

I was never more humbled. After a time of repenting, myself, I again prayed, "Lord, take away the show and teach me to minister in Your love."

I was sincere and God knew it. He answered my prayer.

Sometimes the church is quick to condemn gospel groups that sing in auditoriums where tickets must be sold to support the event. Sadly, most pastors have never counted the cost of what it takes to travel and keep a good group together in a church ministry.

You either go belly-up financially or you go the "auditorium route." There is no middle ground for a professional group.

Unfortunately, this problem does not lie solely with singing ministries. As soon as an evangelist begins to expand and reach out in the world beyond the four walls of the church, when his expenses double, then triple, he finds he must leave the local church and hold his crusades in auditoriums. While an evangelist may use other excuses for leaving the local church, the real reason is that he must move into arenas because local pastors and churches can't control the finances. So the evangelist finds that he must become an independent fund-raiser, always taking his audiences from one financial crisis to another in order to raise enough money to support his ministry. Nothing comes free anymore. The evangelist, or the singer, pays the same for a loaf of bread as anyone else.

Before we can call ourselves a mature church, this is an area that must be corrected. It is an indictment against the local church and against traveling ministries, but in these last days God will bring such harmony to His body that we will trust one another and mature and grow together.

You cannot leave the local church. We had already tried that. While you may do better financially, it is our belief that out there alone, without the covering of the church, you are in far greater danger of becoming weaker. Your danger of getting into error in the Word is greater because your personal life becomes too loose for an effectual witness for the kingdom.

We sang as long as our money held out, but when the money we had accumulated from the concert world was gone, I was forced to come face to face with reality. I sold the bus. It seemed that was becoming a habit. I let the band go and Patty got married and left.

We just stopped singing and said, "Lord, if You want us to sing, we will do it. If You want us to travel, okay. But never again will we travel and pay someone to let us come and sing. You make the way if You want us to go on."

We felt compelled to try again; so I called some of the pastors we had been singing for and told them we had no bus, no band, just Dottie and me and Dottie's guitar. We told them if we sang for them again, we would have to be paid, and our expenses would have to be paid.

Every one of them said the same thing: "We want you to come. We'll pay your air fare and expenses and take care of you. We want your ministry."

Indeed, the sun began shining for us again. God had answered our prayers.

We had never sung with tracks. I wasn't sure we could do a program with just the two of us. Never before had we used a church public address system. And to be honest, the first date we filled, I was scared stiff when just the two of us walked out before the people and began to sing. But by the end of the service, the Holy Spirit had moved in such a way that I knew we were exactly where God wanted us to be.

CHAPTER 18

A Place to Hide

God has peculiar ways of changing our situations. As we were going through our problems, I felt we needed a place to hide. Looking around Nashville for property, I found a 136-acre farm in Pleasant View, twenty-five miles north of the city, and I bought it about the year of 1972. This was when we still had money from the concert singing days.

The farm was perfect for us. It had a beautiful, eight-acre grove of oak trees, some of them 200 years old. To spruce up this small forest we had a bulldozer clear out the underbrush, and in a clearing in the center of the grove, we started building our house that I had designed on three napkins at lunch one day in the Holiday Inn.

Take a bit of advice from me: If you don't love to rake leaves, don't ever build a house in the woods.

The farm had an old empty tennant house. That summer we painted one of the rooms in that house and made a bedroom out of it, so we could stay there and watch our house being built. Since the old house had no city water, I filled a galvanized tub each morning and let the sun warm the water for our baths.

This place was like Heaven to us. We had a lake full of fish, and almost every morning while hammers and saws sounded from the big house going up, we rode our golf cart down to the lake and fished.

Dottie, who had been reluctant to leave the city, became so much in love with the place that she even picked out a tree to be buried under.

We grew almost everything we ate, from Angus cattle to a three-acre garden I tended and the seventy-five fruit trees I planted. So we had our own beef, and we raised hogs for meat. We had apples, peaches, plums, and pears, and gallons of black-berries. Our crops were so bountiful we gave enough stuff away to feed a camp meeting.

Our lives took on new dimensions, the rifts in our marriage were healed, and we lived there in semi-seclusion for seven years.

All that time was a period of healing and growing. God began showing me that I was the priest of our home and family. I had never heard that before. He began teaching me the parallel be-tween husband and wife and His church. Very clearly, He showed me that as Christ made the church His glory, I was to make Dottie my glory.

To become your husband's glory is impossible for the woman to achieve. It is the husband's highest honor to bestow upon whom or what he desires to bestow it. I must work diligently giv-ing honor and glory to the wife as Christ gave His all to bring glory to His church. When a man understands this teaching, all competition is removed. Equal rights between men and women are abolished because no woman would want to descend from the lofty position of being her husband's glory to become a mere equal. This would be too great a letdown.

God worked on Dottie too. He began teaching her that as Sarah made Abraham and called him lord, this was her role. Even as the church made Christ Lord of the heavenly realm, she was to elevate me into the position of lord in our home. No man can make himself lord over his wife. That is a position of honor that can only be given through love.

It is no hard matter to give your wife love, honor, and glory when you understand Christ's love for His church. It is not difficult for a woman to make her husband lord of their home when she understands making Christ Lord of His church.

There on the farm old hurts, old scars, and memories were washed and healed. Our lives became so in tune with God that Dottie and I could sit for hours in perfect peace and solitude.

In our beautiful hideaway there, Dottie vowed that songs grew on trees. It was there that she wrote some of her greatest songs. At her favorite fishing spot, she wrote the children's musicals *Down by the Creekbank* and most of the songs for *Camp Goo-La-Mock-ee*.

CHAPTER 19

Unusual Man

Dottie's father was quite unlike anyone I had ever met. Walking into a strange restaurant, he was so gregarious that he would manage to have a conversation with everyone in it. The man never met a stranger. His name was Jerald Vernon but everyone called him Chick. Chick Luttrell. Often I tell Dottie, she takes after her father in Holy boldness. He had something of a double nature. You'd see him one time and he would act as religious as anyone could be, but the next time you saw him he might be stepping out with another woman. Those latter times were always embarrassing to Dottie.

When we drove to Kentucky to visit Dottie's parents, we never knew whether he would ask us to leave or invite us to go with him to a local revival.

One night we received word that he had been in an automobile wreck and was not expected to live. Some of his bones were crushed, several ribs were broken, he had a concussion, and was in a coma. We rushed to the hospital to be by his side.

After several days he regained consciousness and as we explained his condition to him, he began to weep. Holding Dottie's hand, he looked up at her and said, "Little Dottie, I sure do need to know your God."

There in the hospital, possibly on his death bed, God saved him, and later brought him out of the hospital. He lived nine more years and he would come to our meetings and stand with his hand toward Heaven, testifying of God's saving grace. He became a warrior for the Lord.

He was the first of Dottie's parents to pass over. Dottie's mother lived with us then for several years, but now she is also gone.

"She was my best friend," Dottie says unabashedly.

We are so blessed to have had the tremendous experience of knowing our parents. My mother passed away several years ago. She was my kind of saint. When in church she stood to testify, the church became silent, because Aunt Mary was testifying and you could believe that what Aunt Mary said came from God.

My father lived to be ninety-two, and he was born fifty years too soon. Years ago, he believed many things about the kingdom, prosperity, sowing seeds, divine health, things like that that the Church laughed at then but now preaches.

When his time to die came, he said, "I'm going to die at home like a man." His children all gathered around. He looked at each of us and told us he had no pain, then smiled, waved goodbye, and, looking up toward Heaven, died.

When your parents are gone, a strange, lonely feeling comes over you. At those times, Dottie's phrase—"You're nobody's child"—really fits. In time, you can look back and no longer feel the hurt so badly, and only good memories remain. Our mind then seems like a computer, sorting through the files, discarding faults, failures, and shortcomings, and all that remains are the pleasant things you remember.

May the legacy we leave behind be filled with the same joy in the hearts of those we love.

CHAPTER 20

Elvis

Of all the friends we've made over the years, the most unique was Elvis Presley, who was without question one of a kind. He became a very personal friend of the Rambos. We would spend days at a time with him in Las Vegas and Lake Tahoe, Nevada.

We met Elvis about eighteen years before his death, back in the fifties, and he loved gospel music so much that he would often tell us, "They've set me up on a pedestal and I can't get off of it. If I could go back and do it over, I would sing just gospel music." But, of course, he couldn't go back.

The night we met him, he came to the National Quartet Convention and his people set up a tent-like structure to hide him in backstage. The structure was so angled that he could see the stage but no one could see him.

When we finished singing, the concert promoter asked us if we'd like to meet Elvis.

"Yeah, I'd like to," I said, and the girls agreed.

He introduced us and our relationship began to grow immediately. We all hit if off. We spoke the same language, and we genuinely liked him.

For the next eighteen years we would visit Elvis two or three times a year. This was a great respite for us. It gave us some quality time away from what we were doing, and it always seemed to refresh us. We would go see him for a week at a time, either in Las Vegas or elsewhere. We would stay with his group and he would take care of us—see that we got good seats at his shows, sing with us, and spend a lot of time with us just talking. He took our albums with him on the road and listened to them. To me, that was a great compliment for gospel.

Dottie always said Elvis was incredibly gifted. He was also very honest and generous. But Dottie thought he was a runaway boy—that he was running away from God. We would minister to him and he'd say, "I love God. I know God."

There have been so many books written about Elvis by so many different people that we have been very cautious in even mentioning his name, lest we join the "Make-A-Buck-Off-Elvis Club."

We enjoyed a relationship with him that few ever knew.

When we went to visit him, armed guards escorted us to his personal dressing room, and just before show time, they would take us out to Elvis's private table where we would enjoy his show with his friends. After the show, Elvis would want to sing gospel music for a couple of hours, and then we would sit and talk for hours.

Elvis was accustomed to buying everyone and when he tried to give us a new car and we refused, he didn't know how to deal with it. Everyone constantly tried to get things from him, it seemed, and he built up such a defense around himself that few people came to know the real person.

Once when we were visiting him, he found out that it was Dottie's birthday. He sneaked up behind her and put a gorgeous necklace around her neck and told her, "Happy Birthday, Dottie."

That afternoon when we started to leave, Elvis told us, "Somebody's always trying to get me to sell or give them one of my jump suits, but I never have." He went into a huge dressing closet, pulled his favorite stage costume from the rack and gave it to Dottie. "I want you to have that one," he said. "It's the one I wore to film my Hawaiian special in." She treasures that. Since his death, many museums and all sorts of people have tried to buy it—even rent it—but it is too personal for us to ever part with it, if only temporarily. It's quite showy, and it's still very precious to Dottie.

Elvis was like a brother to Dottie, the type of brother she never had. Her brothers left home so young that she wasn't around them a lot. Elvis loved and respected our family just as a brother of Dottie's would.

About four o'clock one morning when we still sat up talking in Elvis's suite in the Las Vegas Hilton, Elvis wanted to go down to the stage and clown around. On stage, we were having a good time, just being silly, and suddenly I took a good look at the life-sized statues of women around the room, all dressed in hoopskirts and other *Gone with the Wind* paraphernalia, and I asked Elvis why all the statues were white.

"They should have made at least one black," I told him.

He stopped and looked from statue to statue, and suddenly he smiled like a pixie with the corner of his mouth turning slightly upward. "You want one of 'em black?" he said. "Let's make one black."

Elvis's bodyguard, Red, who had come downstairs with us, climbed over the wire-caged area that housed the supplies, and handed out a step ladder and a gallon of black paint and a paint brush.

That's how one of those ladies, at four A.M., suddenly became black: Elvis and I painted her black.

The next night on stage, Elvis stopped the show, had the spotlight put on the mannequin, and told how she had suddenly become black.

Often Dottie and I would talk to Elvis about the Lord, and in his own way Elvis loved God.

He always asked us to pray with him, and we always did.

Elvis hated phony people, and he did love real Christians.

He would have loved nothing better than to be able to go to church and be himself, but he told me that the last time he went to church in Memphis, women almost tore his clothes off him.

Once in Las Vegas, on the night before his girlfriend's birthday, Elvis waited till four o'clock in the morning, then ventured downstairs in the hotel to the jewelry store, which was located beside the elevator. He thought he could get in there unnoticed and buy his girlfriend a present. But some women saw him and word spread and other women converged quickly on the jewelry shop and literally tore most of his clothes off him before he could get back in the elevator. It is hard for some people to understand the appeal he had to women. Christian or not, it didn't seem to matter, they all acted just alike. He had an awesome power about him to draw people.

Just a few months before Elvis died, we went to see him. He was beginning to look bad, gaining a lot of weight. He was eating when we got there and Dottie sat down beside him and couldn't help staring at him, I suppose, because he had changed so much.

"What are you looking at?" he demanded.

"Elvis," she said, "I've been having some strange feelings about you. Your health is bad."

Among his other problems, he had a lot of colon trouble.

"I've really been praying for you," she said, "and I really wish you would take better care of yourself."

As she sat there, a strange feeling came over her, a feeling that she might never see him again. She didn't mention that to him, but she said, "Before we leave today, I want to hold your hand and say an extra prayer." They sat there and talked about the Lord. We always seemed to talk about the Lord, and songwriting, and gospel music. He loved to sing gospel, and in his suite, we'd gather around the piano and sing it. That afternoon Dottie prayed a long time with him and he sat there and held her hand and cried like a little boy.

Her intuition was right. She never saw him again. Dottie had been working in the studio, cutting a solo album, the day Elvis died. She had finished and was in her car, pulling out of the studio lot, when word came over the radio that Elvis was dead. She stopped the car and cried for him.

They really were very close, Dottie and Elvis. They had a common prayer time—nine in the morning. When he could, he

145

would telephone her and they would pray together over the phone. When he couldn't, they still prayed at nine o'clock. They would write out prayer requests on pieces of paper and trade them, and then they could pray for the same things at the same time.

"So much of what's been written about Elvis is not true," Dottie says. "We knew the real Elvis, and he was genuine. He loved his mother, loved his little girl. I've never known a boy ever to love like Elvis did. His father, Vernon, was a dear friend of our family, and Elvis loved him very much. I didn't know Elvis's mother, but felt I did because he talked about her so much."

A few months before he died, Elvis wanted to do a tribute to Dottie by recording an entire album of her songs. We had already signed the contract for the publishing when he passed away. He recorded one of Dottie's songs, "If That Isn't Love," that was released on an album called *Good Times*.

We miss Elvis so much. Not the on-stage, showbiz personality, but the little boy Elvis, the kind-hearted, everloving Elvis. He wasn't always perfect, but we didn't care. He was Elvis.

Maybe when he walks up to God, and God sees things that aren't perfect, He'll just say, "Oh, that's all right; that's just Elvis."

CHAPTER 21

Sojourn in Los Angeles

When Reba and Dony McGuire told us they wanted to get married, I was much more calm than the first time she wed. I said, "I spent seventeen thousand dollars on your first wedding, and this one is going to be different."

We all flew to Las Vegas, checked into a couple of suites at the Hilton, and then went down to one of the wedding chapels on The Strip for the ceremony.

We intended to keep the wedding a secret for a few months, but wouldn't you know that when we walked into the wedding chapel, the minister ran up to us and said, "Well, praise the Lord, if it ain't the Singing Rambos!"

By the time we got back to Nashville, the whole world knew about the wedding.

Dony came from a good family. He was the last of seven children born to Mac and Mabel McGuire in Tulsa, Oklahoma. He studied music from the age of five, and through his growing years, he and his four brothers, Robert, Ronnie, Jerry, and Jack, traveled with and sang for their preacher father. They had a tough time, too. Sometimes they would drive slowly along the road, picking up pop bottles, which they cashed in and used the money for gasoline to get home.

Fate struck Dony a cruel blow in February of 1961 when he was nine. The McGuire family was enjoying lunch with a family from their church when Dony went out to ride his bicycle. He was hit by a car and was in a coma for two days. When he woke up, he found that his left arm had been crushed so badly that he would probably never use it again, and that his left leg had been ripped off his body by the car.

But by persistently hard work and a mother who would not let him quit, Dony regained the use of his arm and hand, and with an artificial limb he gets around as well as anyone. He even came back from the accident to play baseball again, making all-star teams and playing for tournament championship teams.

After that he went into music in a big way. He sang with the Gardner Family of California at the National Quartet Convention in October of 1969, and afterward received various offers to sing professionally. That December, he joined the Downings and began not only to sing professionally but to cut his teeth on writing, publishing, arranging, and producing music.

In the mid-1970s Dony found himself in the middle of a failing marriage and using drugs and alcohol to keep going. His divorce was painful, and afterward Dony pressed himself to the limits, publishing and producing recordings. He produced fifty records a year which left him little time to sleep and do other things, and he reached deeper into drugs and alcohol to keep going.

When he and Reba married, we had no idea he was into drugs and drinking as deeply as he was. He had a beautiful little girl named Dionne. What a joy it was for us when Reba, Dony, and Dionne came out to the farm. We fished, swam, and just goofed off. Everything appeared to be coming up roses for all of us, and we just settled into a good family routine and thought, "This is really home!"

But things weren't as rosy for Reba and Dony as we thought. They weren't having trouble, nothing like that. They came to us one evening and dropped a bombshell.

"There is so much opposition to our marriage here in Nashville," Reba said, "that we have decided to move to California." There was a lot of opposition to two divorcees getting married, opposition that came both from the Church and the world of gospel music.

Before we fully realized what was happening, they were gone— and that's when God began shaking our nest.

God doesn't always talk to me, but one day as I was out walking on the farm, He spoke in a way that was almost frightening. He said, "I'm going to take the love of this place from you, and I want you to begin pointing your ministry toward the West Coast."

That incident was rather like having a prayer go unanswered. When God answers a prayer with a "no," we sometimes think He hasn't answered at all, but He has. To move to California was definitely not what I wanted, but I knew God meant business. At that time, the West Coast was almost like a mission field to us. Every time we went there, we came home broke and disgusted. We had always complained about how hard it was to minister there.

When I told Dottie what God had said, I felt for the first time a sense of rebellion in her. Very definitely, she did not want to go. But in 1981 we went anyway. We closed the house and rented a house in Beverly Hills, the old Jean Harlow house; rented enough furniture to get by and began chipping away at Satan's grip on the West Coast.

Larry Gatlin wrote a song that says, "California's a brand new game," and this is really true. California is hard to describe. Los Angeles, for example, is not just a city; it's a county joined to other counties, and there are hundreds of cities linked together, making one vast sea of people.

With exceptions, most churches in L.A. are relatively small, containing up to four hundred members. Talk about a mission field!

But to really get into our work, we had to overcome a recognition problem. We had been singing all our lives, and in the beginning churches we went to in California had only a handful of members who'd ever heard of the Rambos. Maybe twenty percent of the membership had an acquaintance, however vague, with us. We were not accustomed to that, and it deflated our egos. At times, we felt we were starting all over again.

To draw a crowd to these churches at any time besides Sunday morning was a real task. So we made our first visits on Sunday morning, and then after the congregation had heard us sing we could come in on a weekday evening and expect to draw a fairly good crowd.

California bears no resemblance to the Bible Belt. Every culture under the sun lives there. We had to spend a lot of preparation time on this ministry, but in the end it was worth it, because God honored it.

After we became established there, some of our best times, some of our greatest services were on the West Coast. We could work full-time in the city of Los Angeles and never run out of places to minister. There were many good things about it, too. We could sing every night and not have to spend those endless hours and days on the road. We could be home every night!

Also, if we could fully utilize the television market everywhere like Paul and Jan Crouch have used it in Los Angeles with their Trinity Broadcasting Television Network, just think of the great works that could be done in cities like New York. It is no wonder Satan tries to present such a distorted view of television ministries. But this area is still relatively new to the church world, and we are still learning, all of us.

Because of a great and debilitating illness Dottie is going through, we have been invited to appear on television many times recently to talk about the war we are fighting with pain, and after each appearance we receive hundreds of letters. Without opening the envelopes, I can tell you how ninety percent will read. The first paragraph will tell of seeing us and will mention that they are praying for us. But in the following pages they tell of the pain and hurts they are going through. Then we certainly pray for them.

We live in a hurting world, and most people feel that nobody cares. They search for someone who will listen. Most of the support for Christian television comes from people who are searching for someone to simply say, "We care." What an opportunity just to be able to go into homes of strangers and love them, pouring in oil and wine.

We met a lot of fine Christian people in California. One was Cynthia Karraker. Her husband died a few years ago with AIDS. He was music director of a well-known church. Since his death, we have watched Cynthia's growth in Christ, and the development of a great ministry to people with AIDS and their families.

What a lady of courage! But it is sad to say that when she contacts pastors across America, many refuse to even pray for those dying of AIDS. They are afraid, or too busy, lifting up their religious robes and walking around the issue. Some of them say, "God doesn't want the world ministering to the hopeless." Just in case no one has mentioned lately, Jesus sends His Church to minister to those without hope. But God is doing a brand-new thing. He will bypass the pulpit if He has to and raise up saints from the pews to do the work He has called the Church to do.

If you have AIDS, if you're a homosexual, a lesbian, if you're a drug addict, remember Jesus came to seek and to save the lost. He loves you even if no one tells you. He still cares about you.

I will praise the Church for its mighty works. While the religious world may be floundering trying to find itself, God has a Church that is victorious and is maturing and becoming salt and light.

After forty years of ministry, I feel I am qualified to point out our high points and also state the areas where God must still refine us. After all, He is not yet finished with His Church. We are still maturing. The bride is not yet grown. Sometimes I think we're still in pigtails, but, never fear, we are still the apple of His eye!

Trinity Broadcasting Television Network opened its arms to us. We were on Trinity almost every week. I hosted the main show a lot, a talk show. Dottie cut a series of television shows called *Dottie Rambo Magazine,* and we began working churches, mostly in the Los Angeles area. If a church had five members and asked us to sing, we sang. It took a lot of hard work because we were plowing hard but fertile ground, but within a year our ministry had grown tremendously in a place that seemed impossible.

Dottie's show, a thirty-minute weekly show, became one of Trinity's top programs. She usually had a cooking segment in which she cooked a real dish. She had guests like Barbara Mandrell and Dottie West, and a lot of other well-known music people. They would sing and we would sing, and Dottie would talk to them, and the show was relaxed and very popular.

At times, living in Beverly Hills, I felt like one of the Beverly Hillbillies. I don't know which one, Jed or Jethro! Maybe a little of both. What was an old country boy from Kentucky doing in that place?

We lived in the Harlow house about a year, and from it we could walk right down to Rodeo Drive. The house was old, two-story, with three bedrooms, a living room, dining room, kitchen, breakfast room, a sunroom, and three baths. It had gorgeous ceilings and hardwood floors and was what you would expect in Jean Harlow's time to have been very elegant.

"It was really a neat feeling just to be in that house," Dottie said, "because Jean Harlow was quite a lady; I mean, with her reputation, her acting ability, and her beauty. I looked for things that would remind me of her. Certain tiles in the floor looked like they would have been chosen by a woman, and, of course, she had chosen them."

There were a lot of stories in that house. Going into it, there were little folios with pictures on them, telling all about the house, when it was built, how long Harlow lived there, all like that. So it was legitimate. It had indeed been hers. She was killed in 1937 at the age of twenty-six.

Eventually we bought a house in Orange County and settled there. We liked it. The climate was beautiful. We began to think maybe this was home. Our Orange County house was a ranch-style house on one-and-a-half acres. California is unique; if you have an acre-and-a-half, your place is zoned as a ranch and you can keep a horse. I got a kick out of the thought that my calf lot back in Tennessee was larger than my ranch in California. Our place in California was on the side of a hill and we had thirty or forty fruit trees and a little barn, but no horse.

Reba and Dony lived about an hour north in Chatsworth, up in the valley. In Los Angeles distance is measured by time rather than mileage. We managed to see them often, and after a while, we began to suspect that all was not right with them. Then we began to fear that something was definitely wrong. We had heard about Dony's problems with alcohol and drugs, but like so many others do, we chose to stick our heads in the sand. We told ourselves if we didn't notice it, maybe it would go away.

But it didn't. It grew worse until Reba called one night and asked me to come and get her. When I reached her house, Dony, in a drunken rage, had ordered her out of the house and piled all her clothes in the middle of the street.

She moved in with us.

Dony phoned me several nights later and said, "Dad, I've got to have some help. Will you help me?" His tongue was thick and I knew he was loaded. But I also knew he was beginning to realize that he did, indeed, need help.

I drove to his house as fast as I could, and he was so out of it that he couldn't even talk. Quickly I took him to a local alcohol treatment center. Later, we found that he was consuming a fifth and a half of vodka and some amount of narcotics every day.

He was submissive, almost eager to be treated. We heard of a treatment center in Atlanta that was supposedly the best, and we made arrangements for Dony to enter it. Knowing we couldn't trust him alone on the plane with alcohol so available, I went with him.

I couldn't stay in Atlanta because we had our work on the West Coast, and that's when the Chapel Hill Harvester Church of Atlanta stepped in. Bishop Earl Paulk, a Godly man, pastored it. The church surrounded Dony with love and wouldn't let go— not that he or any of us wanted it to turn him loose. Every time Dony looked up, he said later, there was Pastor Dwayne Swilley coming to be with him.

With the help of this church and his counselors at the treatment center, Dony made good progress, and when he was finally released, he was convinced that he had to have a home church like Chapel Hill. He was also convinced that he must have a strong spiritual covering, else Satan would come back and cause his feet to stumble again.

As a family, we learned about alcoholism and drug addiction being a sickness, a disease, not simply just a sin. Dony had trouble admitting he was an alcoholic, but like a man, he finally stood up and faced his problem, admitted it, and then turned to God for deliverance.

He and Reba were back together then, and it was at that time that they decided to move to Atlanta and associate themselves with the Chapel Hill Harvester Church, which had really been a lifesaver for Dony.

After seeing how much the church meant to both Dony and Reba, and noticing the great difference the church had made in their lives, Dottie and I began to discuss whether we should also move to the Atlanta area.

To be perfectly honest, Dottie, Reba, and Dony started discussing our moving there. The last place on earth I would have chosen to live was Atlanta.

But Dottie had an answer for my arguments against living in Atlanta. She said, "So what? I felt the same about L.A."

I had no answer to that argument, and out of desperation I prayed, "God, if you want us to move to Atlanta, give me a buyer for the house and farm in Nashville, a buyer for this house in California, and You pick out the house You want us to have in Atlanta. Only then will I know this is Your will."

God certainly spoke back to me that time. Within three weeks—this was in 1985—we had sold the farm in Nashville and had a firm offer for the house in Los Angeles. We came to Atlanta looking for a house, and when we drove up with a real estate agent in front of a beautiful home in Stone Mountain, near Atlanta, God spoke very clearly to me and said, "This is the one I've picked out for you."

We were so near Stone Mountain, the largest piece of granite in the United States, that I could walk to it.

Dottie immediately claimed a small room just off our bedroom, and said she would do her writing in it. We rushed back to L.A., loaded up our furniture, and headed for Atlanta. While we were on the road, a friend went by the empty house we were moving into, and as he walked up the steps, he said he heard voices coming from Dottie's writing room. Expecting to find a prowler, he opened the door to the room and saw huge gothic angels dancing in a circle, carrying silver trays, and on these trays were music notes and lyrics. One of the angels said, "I can't wait for her to get here and put all these notes together so we'll know what they sound like."

So this room—we called it the "Angel Room"—was where Dottie went to commune with the Lord, and in this room Dottie wrote many of her latest songs.

CHAPTER 22

Grandkids!

Late one afternoon Reba and Dony came in our house carrying roses and said they had an announcement to make. The first thing I thought was, *Well, here goes—they're moving again!* But I missed the mark, and I was shocked when Reba said, "I'm pregnant." She had been told by five different specialists that she could never birth children, even though she had gone through two corrective surgeries.

Everyone who knew all of us had been praying for Reba to have a child, and different ministries had prophesied that she would. But to me, the shock of our little girl going to have a baby was awesome. My thoughts kept running back to when Reba herself was a little baby, and I almost cried.

Months before that, Reba had told us that she would have a little boy some day and that she was to name him Israel Anthem. Dottie had had a dream about the same thing: She dreamed she was singing, "Dance for me, Israel," and he would spin like a top. So we had no doubt that Reba's baby would be a boy.

Reba had decided she would have natural childbirth, and Judy Sproles, one of her dearest friends, became her coach. It seemed to us that every time we saw Reba she was sprawled out on the floor, puffing away, doing Lamaze exercises.

Reba also said she believed that since the church was maturing, women should have children without medication.

Dottie rolled her eyes at me and said, "Yeah, sure! You just go for it. We're behind you." And she couldn't help snickering.

When Reba's time came and she went to the hospital to have the baby, it looked like a television production. There were a dozen people in the room, and we had a television camera set up to film the entire procedure. Things went smoothly for a while.

And then, as Reba's time neared, we watched the countenance change on this spiritual child of ours. Suddenly she was complaining about everyone's perfume, even the Juicy Fruit® gum someone was chewing.

Great beads of sweat appeared on her forehead, and Reba looked for Dottie and said, "Mama, maybe I had better have just a tiny shot of medicine."

As time passed, and the doctor was ordering, "Push! Push!" Reba's eyes bulged and she screamed, "I want drugs!"

When the baby was born, a beautiful, black-haired, little girl, it appeared that she raised her head as if to say, "Hello, world."

Everyone was so happy, but no one knew what to name her. No one had picked a name for a girl. Then Brother Paulk came to our rescue and said, "Her name should be Destiny, because she is destined for the ministry, and she should also carry the Rambo name since she is a fifth generation of ministry."

So Reba and Dony named her Destiny Rambo McGuire.

Dottie and I would like to publicly apologize to every grandparent we have made fun of in the past. We did not understand that grandchildren fill a void in your life, a void you probably don't even know is there.

The next two years were filled with the love of this little girl who called us "Bam-Buck" and "Dan-Dot." She would tell everybody she was "Bam-Buck's Angle." She couldn't say "angel."

To us, it was a mystery why God had given Reba a name for a boy and preachers had prophesied and Grand Dot had dreamed about a boy. But it was no mystery to Reba. She continued to proclaim she was going to have a son.

Sure enough, along came this bald-headed little boy who looked like a candidate for some football team's backfield. He was named Israel Anthem McGuire, and he captivated all of our hearts.

Israel and Destiny are opposites. Destiny is petite and full of pep. Israel, with broad shoulders, is laid back and gentle, but very strong.

They each have an anointing given from birth that we believe will do great works for the Lord.

A few years ago a prophetic word was spoken over Dony and Reba's ministry. The word was that "God was placing a mantle of ministry on them to lead the church into warfare music."

I will be the first to say I did not fully understand this, but I watched them proceed as though the church fully understood their message. Writing great songs of battle, victorious statements like "The Champion Has Come" and "Ready for Battle," this came at the forefront of a great battle Dottie and I were just entering into—the battle of Dottie's illness.

Since then I have watched God working with great ministries, and today the bookshelves and sermons are filled with topics of "Spiritual Warfare." This should be of no surprise to the Church because in Old Testament times, God often sent singers, praisers, and dancers in front of the army. This definitely has been the case with the ministry of Reba and Dony, leading the Church in warfare ministry. It isn't just a case of singing and preaching about the Sweet By-and-By and Won't-it-be-wonderful-there, because God doesn't want His Church to just think about Over-in-the-Glory-Land; He is interested in his Church developing and maturing into that grand and glorious Church without spot or wrinkle.

Speaking for herself and Dony, Reba describes their ministry this way:

"The main mission Dony and I felt were several prophetic words that were spoken over us, like 'I'm going to do a resurrection in you and create a whole new ministry,' and 'I'm putting a warfare mantle on you.' God said, 'I want you to teach my people that this is a fight, a war, and I've given them weapons and strategies.' He said to teach His people that it is a fixed fight, that Jesus had already won the victory, and we had to learn to walk under it.

"Then God began saying strange things to us, that he wanted us to comfort the afflicted with the same comfort we had been comforted with. He didn't stop there, but also said, 'Not only do I want you to comfort the afflicted, but I want you to afflict the comfortable. When you sing it's going to be as if there are thumbtacks in every chair. The church has been a sleeping giant and I want you to wake it up and get it in the war.' "

They minister not only to the sick and afflicted, but to barren women and to those whose marriages are on the rocks. They have written testimonies from more than two hundred barren women who became pregnant. They say to those struggling in marriage, "If God can heal our marriage and work in it, He can heal any marriage." Reba shares with the sick how she was cured of meningitis, and how Dony's broken arm was healed after being shattered in fourteen places between the elbow and wrist. They tell how Dony's mother was a prayer warrior who refused to give up. "She just kept on bombarding heaven with her prayers," Reba said, "and now Dony's right hand works just like the left."

They tell people that God is a God who heals people. "We just take what we know, what God has shown us, and teach it to others," Reba said. "You can't teach what you don't know yourself. We have not worked so much with the lost as with those who are broken of body. God wants a body that is good and strong; so we've taken the Good News to those people. And we've taken the fight to the church, raising up an army with God using us to be the trumpet cry. That's what He told us to do."

I marvel at Dony's ministry. I marvel at the Grace of God when I think about scooping up the fragments of Dony's broken life, destroyed by drink and drugs, and bringing him to Atlanta, and now to see him touching the lives of thousands. By the Grace of God, Dony also became the son we never had.

And when I see my baby, Reba, and watch the Holy Spirit lead her into depths of worship and ministry I never dreamed possible, I stand amazed. If we've ever done one thing right, it was to give the world a Reba. And when Dottie and I are gone, the greatest legacy we could ever leave behind is this child filled with grace and truth to sing of God's mighty power.

The purifying process these two have and are going through will produce great fruit that will continue to grow through Destiny, Israel, and Dionne.

I've watched them go forth and sing 374 services in one year. I've seen them work in mission fields where they didn't make enough to buy the diesel fuel for their bus. But because there is such ministry burning within them, they, like their parents before them, had no choice but to go where God said go.

Someone asked if we had it to do all over again, would we do it. We answered, "Yes, only with more vigor." God never fails.

CHAPTER 23

Mission Work

Each year the Rambos tried to take at least one mission tour overseas. We have ministered in perhaps thirty countries—all over Europe, Asia, the Caribbean, Mexico, South America—and every time we did a mission tour, we wanted to double our efforts because of the spiritual hunger throughout the world.

We did five television network specials in Holland one year. Television in Holland is not like here. When you're on television there, you're it. Nothing else is on. It's a state television station and is the only one in the country. On many American stations, you go in the TV station, turn on the lights and cameras, and do a television show in a few hours. It isn't that way in Holland. They use a whole week putting a special together, building elaborate sets, getting everything just right, rehearsing and rehearsing some more. They spend a lot of money and do a great job. During those times, we would walk down the street in Amsterdam and people would point to us and say, "Boock and Dotie!"

We have toured Belgium, Sweden, Denmark, and Germany, working in a lot of churches. We did a show in an American military base in Weisbaden, Germany. In the 1970s we did two tours to that part of the world and thoroughly enjoyed both.

The biggest part of our missions work has been in the United States, but we also made two tours of the Caribbean, first in 1980 and next in 1986.

One of the trips was to the Caribbean Islands of Dominica, Barbados, and Saint Kitts-Nevis.

Most Americans find it difficult to understand the importance of Christian radio, especially in Third World countries. On most of the smaller islands in the Caribbean there is little or no television, but all have strong Christian radio stations, and for years these stations had played our records. We found it a strange experience to be riding in a taxi and hear the radio announcer suddenly say, "Here are Buck and Dottie Rambo to sing. . . ." For the first time in my life I wanted to scream out, "Hey! That's us!"

The first island we visited was Dominica, and the landing there was hairy. Our small plane approached the densely covered island and headed for a mountainside. I could not believe we were actually going to land on the side of a mountain, but as we approached the hillside we suddenly rounded it and a small landing strip came into view.

When we were safely on the ground, several pastors and a representative of the Christian radio station came out to greet us. Their greeting was so joyous, you'd have thought the Apostle Paul had come.

A few years ago, a hurricane destroyed almost all the buildings on Dominica. Everywhere we went, we saw people living inside three small walls with a roof of tin. Poverty was rampant, but our driver happily informed us that no one on the island went hungry. Because of the rich volcanic soil and the heavy, fertile jungle, ample food supplies were grown.

We did several concerts and a Sunday church service on the island. We thought their singing and music would reflect the old-fashioned church, but not so. They were very advanced, charismatic in their worship, and "Kingdom Now" in their doctrine. I stood in amazement and listened to the pastor preach a sermon that would have made Bishop Earl Paulk proud.

We then visited Barbados where the Rev. Cuke was pastor.

Since we had been there before, thousands of friends greeted us. What a beautiful people, and what a beautiful island!

Saint Kitts-Nevis came next. These were islands Christopher Columbus visited on his second voyage to the New World. He originally named the island Saint Christopher, but the British started their first Caribbean colony there and renamed the island Saint Kitts.

On these islands, things were different. Trinity Broadcasting had a television station there and almost everyone had a TV set. We had been on television there so much that everywhere we went, people called us by name, even in the downtown shopping areas.

My heart was heavy, and I knew Dottie's was too, when we left the islands. I would like to have stayed. The beauty of these islands is unbelievable, and the people are great. I promised myself that someday we would return. When we finally get around to ruling and reigning, maybe my reigning will be in Barbados. That would be all right with me.

CHAPTER 24

Disaster

Disaster struck us in October of 1986, just after we returned home from the West Indies. We had emptied and refilled our suitcases and had flown to California for the TBN Fall Telethon. As we were singing on the telethon, Dottie suddenly winced and gasped with a tremendous pain in her lower back. We managed to finish and get off stage and she collapsed in a chair. She said it felt as if someone had hit her a sharp blow—she hadn't strained or twisted her back—and we thought she was having a kidney-stone attack.

She drank a lot of water the rest of the day, but when she woke up the next morning the pain was still there, and still just as severe. Something was protruding from her back, and she said it felt like knives sticking in her. When she twisted or turned she screamed in pain.

We flew back to Atlanta and on our first night at home, the pain was so intense I had to take Dottie to the emergency room at St. Joseph's Hospital twice for shots. The second time we went, they just checked her into the hospital.

After many tests—MRI, CAT scan, moligram, and x-rays—the doctor came in with a grim face and gave us a tremendously dis-

couraging report. He showed us where two spinal discs had cal-
cified and ruptured, forming an S-shaped spur like a knife-blade.
Every time Dottie moved, this spur cut at her spinal cord. The
only way to reach the disc safely and remove it, the physician
said, was to remove her lower left rib and come in from the side.
Because of the danger involved, he said, Dottie must have the
operation or risk paralysis, or even death.

It appeared that Satan had launched an all-out attack against
us; so we got on the phone and called many great ministers and
had them pray for Dottie. When Brother Kenneth Hagin, a supreme evangelical preacher, phoned and began praying with
Dottie, the entire telephone system in the hospital blew out.

We almost lost Dottie in the hospital. The morphine pump installed after the surgery malfunctioned and a doctor gave her a
bolo shot, which caused her to overdose. Feverishly they worked
over her and in a little while she came around.

The warfare that took place in that hospital was awesome, but
even in her worst pain, Dottie continued to witness. The word
of knowledge would move in her as she ministered to the nurses
and several were saved during this period. Her room was always
busy with nurses coming in, just to let Dottie minister to them.

For twenty-eight days I stayed with Dottie in the hospital.
When she was discharged, one doctor said, "Because the disc
did so much damage to the spinal area, she will always have this
pain."

They tried spinal blocks, different devices and treatments, but
the pain remained intense twenty-four hours a day. We would sit
up in bed night after night, crying and praying for daylight to
come, hoping that perhaps with the new day someone would find
an answer for Dottie's pain.

This went on for thirteen months. We could do nothing. I
closed down our ministry, sold one of our cars, put our house up
for sale, and tried to economize in every way, trying just to survive financially. Some people sent us money, and an appeal by
Brother Paulk brought in around $17,000. This helped, of
course, but our medical expenses were tremendous.

Finally Dottie could stand the terrible routine no more, and she made a decision. "Maybe if I go back to work," she said, "under the anointing I will get my healing."

We went out for four or five dates and tried to minister, and the experience was awesome. Dottie's pain was severe as she got up to speak, and as she ministered people would be healed. We had never seen our services so powerful, but at the end of each service I would have to help her get to bed. I began to wonder why Dottie, too, couldn't be healed.

On our last date, she collapsed and I brought her home in a wheelchair.

During this early time in Dottie's illness, Kenneth Copeland told her that Satan's attack was so fierce, the only way we could combat it, was to stay absolutely in the Word, and to do this we had to keep it playing on cassette in our house every waking hour. If we didn't, he said, the pain would kill Dottie.

We played Bible tapes, preaching tapes, singing tapes, and our church sent us videos of every service.

I abandoned any activities that would take my focus off ministering to Dottie. Every morning when the average person went off to work, we went off to war.

Satan even sent spirits to our home in human form. He did everything he could do to cause confusion. Eventually I had to stop anyone from ministering directly to Dottie except those the Holy Spirit directed through me. I discovered that being lord or priest of my home sometimes meant making difficult decisions, but Dottie was in such pain that I made them.

When you're wrestling on the level of pain that Dottie was on, you become extremely sensitive, extremely attuned to what's happening, not only in the flesh but in everything. There were times (and this may sound weird) that I couldn't listen to the songs of some people in gospel music whom I love very much. It wasn't that they were bad people, or bad songs, but they were just not tuned into where we were.

There were also several televangelists we just couldn't listen to at that time. There was something about where they were in their spirit life that would not bear witness with us. They became so depressing, we couldn't listen to them.

This was when we were introduced to the ministry of Malcolm Smith, who is probably one of the greatest Bible teachers I've ever heard. He holds a lot of seminars for ministers. When he sent us his teachings on the Blood Covenant, it elevated us into a higher dimension of truth; and at last count, Dottie had listened to this six-tape series twenty-five times.

Malcolm Smith is from England and is one of the greatest Bible teachers in the world today. He is accepted not only in the Pentecostal world but in the entire denominational world. Many great pastors and teachers get what they teach from Malcolm. Most preachers get what they teach from somebody. The majority of the charismatic doctrinal teachings taught today come directly from Malcolm Smith, and he says he gets it from somebody else—a lot of it from ancient books.

There was a Chinese preacher named Watchman Nee who has been dead for years and years but whose books are still around, the most fantastic books you'll ever read. Read his books today and you'll say, "He must have written this last week," because it is so in tune with what's happening in the world today.

Some preachers were before their time, and one reason I think that is because they put it in book form, and today, a hundred or more years later, we're reading what those people wrote, what they saw then in the Spirit.

During that period when we discovered Malcolm Smith, we were ministered to by a lot of great men of God—Kenneth Copeland, Billy Graham—I could name many, but some were just not on the same wave length with us. Now that we've emerged from that period, we can listen to those preachers and singers again and enjoy them.

We went through a two-year period in which there was no way I could describe the pain Dottie was going through. For months, she could sleep no more than thirty minutes at a time. We'd sit in bed and the pain would be so bad that water would squirt from her eyes, not drip. It would actually squirt! I would hold her and we would cry and pray for morning because there is something about the night that elevates pain. Often the sun would come up before Dottie closed her eyes in sleep—and that was after taking the heaviest medication that could be given her.

CHAPTER 25

Ordeals in Multiples

We received a telephone call one morning from Dr. Robert Holcomb of Hamilton, Alabama, who had heard about Dottie's pain problem and wanted to come and see if he could help her. At this point, we were almost desperate, not only because of Dottie's pain but also because our financial condition was in such a state. Our church was holding a special service to help us financially.

Since no other doctor had found a solution, we were at a point of desperation from which we would have let almost anyone treat her. Dr. Holcomb agreed to come to our church and see Dottie after the service. We all gathered in the pastor's office and Dr. Holcomb came in carrying a bag full of magnets.

He used a machine called the Episcan to locate key pain points, and there he would place a magnet about the size of a silver dollar and three times as thick. In a matter of minutes, Dottie began to cry in sheer happiness; her pain level had dropped about forty percent for the first time since surgery.

Dr. Holcomb told us of an invention he had of a magnetic bed that ran off a bus generator. The bed was mounted in a large van, which he brought to our house and left for Dottie to use until he could build a magnetic bed specifically for her. When the bed was ready, he installed it in our home.

Since that first meeting, Dr. Holcomb has become one of our dearest friends. He has driven thousands of miles and spent thousands of dollars to help Dottie, and has never taken a penny for his services. Sometimes, in cases like ours, people reach the point that they think all that doctors are after is their money—but Robert has proven to us—this is not true.

The magnetic bed did not remove the pain, but working in combination with the prescribed medication, it enabled us to better control the pain. Most of the time, it has helped us control the pain without tears and for us this was a miracle.

After a year of almost constant battle, Robert finally told us, "Dottie must have help from another source, perhaps more surgery." We checked with Mayo Clinic, Johns Hopkins, and several pain centers, but we found no encouragement. We felt they gave us the run-around. Spinal cord damage, we have learned, is something most doctors and hospitals shy away from because there is no way to operate on the spinal cord.

For Dottie's surgery, we finally settled on Vanderbilt Hospital in Nashville. After all, this was home. Vanderbilt is a college hospital and research center. Patients are brought there when everyone else gives up on them. Frankly, this was where we felt we were at this time.

A graduate of Vanderbilt University, Dr. Holcomb was on familiar ground. He set up our schedule and suggested we take Dr. Michael McLean as our in-house physician. Dr. McLean is such a personable man, it didn't take long for us to get on a first-name basis, and he is now just "Mike" to us. Too, he and Robert have become great friends, and together, even though tragedy followed, they have become a source of great strength to both Dottie and me. I doubt if we could have survived the next few months had God not placed them in our lives.

The next few weeks were intense times as Dr. McLean called in a team of specialists, and at least a dozen of them went over Dottie carefully. Each of them wanted tests and in their thoroughness, they left no stone unturned.

Medically they were great; but Dottie and I had become keenly aware in St. Joseph's and Vanderbilt, that spirits other than the Holy Spirit were at work.

Finally a Dr. Blumenkoph, a neurosurgeon, met with us and gave us three options.

One was to surgically implant a device in Dottie's brain that would sensor out pain signals.

Two was to put a morphine pump in her side to administer medication directly to her spinal cord.

Three was called the Drez Procedure. In this, they would kill the nerve where it came off the spinal cord, leaving a numbness in a four-inch-wide strip around Dottie's left side. The doctor said this procedure had only about a twenty-five percent success ratio, but we concluded, according to the information given us by the physician, and considering the risk factor, that this was our best alternative.

Had we been given all the facts about side effects, the danger of paralysis of the leg and colon, the tremendous pain that accompanies this procedure, we would not have chosen it. But whether intentional or not—we'll never know—we were given none of these facts. Dr. Blumenkoph did not go into any of this with us.

We have learned since that many neurosurgeons refuse to do this procedure because of the risks involved.

The surgery was scheduled, and Dr. Blumenkoph said it would last about three hours.

Thinking we had made our best decision with the information we had, we put Dottie in the hands of God and prayed for His help.

Brother and Sister L.H. Hardwick, our former pastors at Christ Church in Nashville, came to stay with me in the waiting room, and we talked while the three-hour estimate lengthened to five hours, then six, and then seven.

After eight hours, Dr. Blumenkoph came to the waiting room, his face as pale as a corpse. "I can't get her to breathe," he said, and turned on his heel and went back into surgery. Twenty minutes later he returned, still pale, and said, "She's breathing, but I can't get her to move her left leg," and again he hurried back inside.

He gave us no further information, no explanation, and you must be able to realize how devastated I was.

Fifteen more minutes passed and he returned to tell me that Dottie was being taken to intensive care and he would see her tomorrow. He left quickly, avoiding my questions.

This began the toughest time we had faced yet. Dottie looked like death. When she came to herself, she asked the attending physician whether she was going to make it.

"We don't know," he said. "It doesn't look good." And then he asked, "What can we do to make you more comfortable?"

"Take me somewhere so I can have my family come in and pray for me," she said, "and I want to see my grandbabies."

She was rolled into a room adjoining ICU, and we began our prayer vigil. Destiny and Israel were brought in to see Grand Dot.

For the next seventeen nights, I slept on the floor beside Dottie's bed. We felt that death lurked always in the room and we learned the hard way about spiritual warfare. We sing songs about it. We testify to it. But few have actually engaged in it.

On the morning following surgery, Dottie's sheets were soaked with something sticky. I called for the nurse and she quickly got the surgeon. Dottie's spine was losing fluid in the bed.

The doctor asked me to leave the room. I walked about a block and took a shower, and when I returned the doctor had a surgical sheet spread across Dottie. He had taken the metal clamps out of the incision, which was about eighteen inches long, and was sewing her back up.

Dottie was lying there praising God and speaking in tongues. Later, I learned that he had given her no medication and was using a hook needle. The pain must have been overwhelming, but Dottie said God told her, "Don't cry—just praise me."

The poor doctor appeared to be really frightened, but we believe he was a messenger from Satan sent to distress Dottie.

Afterward, we were told that the stitching had not been properly done and would have to be done over.

172

"Oh, no," Dottie cried, "you're not going to do that to me again, not without medication."

"I gave you medication," the young doctor protested.

"You did not," Dottie accused, and another doctor was quickly called in to do the stitching. He had medication administered to her, and the procedure was not nearly so painful.

For three weeks, Dottie lay on her back, unable to raise her head, unable to use a bedpan, unable to feed herself. Her left side and left leg were paralyzed. When she became nauseous, she threw up in her hair. This beautiful lady was a mess.

She cried and begged God to take her home. She knew her life was gone. Everything they gave her put her in a stupor. We didn't know it at the time, but for the next five years Dottie would be fed many drugs that would steal her gifts, making her forgetful, thick-tongued, and repetitious. It was a terrible nightmare for such a talented lady to endure.

A dear friend, Marilyn Myers, flew from her home in Miami to Nashville to see Dottie and was so appalled she stayed several days, running me out of the room at bedtime so I could get some rest. She stayed with Dottie all night.

Marilyn saved my life, I am sure, and through her help I learned a great truth in ministry: Don't ever ask if there is anything you can do in a time of distress. Just go ahead and do whatever needs to be done. If you didn't feel something needed doing, you wouldn't ask in the first place.

But I was too proud to ask for help.

Truthfully, I shouldn't have had to ask.

CHAPTER 26

Helping Hands

Dottie spent her birthday strapped to a board. I always send Dottie roses on her birthday, but this time I decided I would give her a nice gown. Walking through the store, thinking how tragic it was that Dottie was paralyzed and without a miracle might never walk normally again, I envisioned her in a wheelchair. Satan was really playing mind games with me.

Then the Lord spoke and His words were loud and clear. "Buy her a pair of the highest-heeled dress shoes you can find," He said. So, by faith, that afternoon I went into her room carrying these silver, rhinestone, high-heeled shoes, and for the first time in a long while Dottie laughed aloud. I joined her, and we both felt better, despite the dark circumstances that surrounded us.

Three weeks later her spine stopped leaking, and Dottie began her long battle against the paralysis in her left side and leg.

The hospital's physical therapy department took over at that point and Dottie remained in the hospital for months, working with a young lady named Michelle. Dr. McLean would not let Dottie give up, and would leave his own patients and come to encourage Dottie.

Finally Dottie began to get back the use of her leg. Week by week she grew stronger. New words became important, words like patience, endurance, and perseverance, and every doctor said Dottie was fighting almost impossible odds. However, Faith preaches Good.

Dottie must have learned the meaning of those words well, because she battled like a Trojan woman, and she overcame the paralysis. Finally, her doctors agreed to let her leave the hospital, provided we remained in Nashville.

What a victory! Day after day for the seven months we stayed in Nashville following that surgery, we battled the demons of hell, who constantly snipped at our heels.

The support team God put together for us was wonderful. It included the Hardwicks: Jim Enoch, a layman in Nashville who came almost daily to the hospital; Jerry and Joan McGuire, Dony's brother and his wife; Tim and Dixie McKeithan of the McKeithans; the First Baptist Church, and Two Rivers Baptist Church. It seemed the whole city was lifting us up to the Lord. Pastors from Madisonville, Kentucky, were involved. Jimmie Russell, our former pastor, came and prayed. And the most awesome thing was that, although they had come to minister to Dottie, she found ways to pray for and minister to them.

When finally we were ready to leave Nashville and come home to Atlanta, Drs. Holcomb and McLean sat down with us and Holcomb rededicated himself to Dottie's recovery: "I'll see Dottie Rambo walk again if it's the last thing I do on earth."

Dr. McLean seconded the statement.

After meeting these two men, my idea of a Christian has changed a bit. I have never known any two men who genuinely cared more about humanity and were more willing to give of themselves than these two physicians. They don't always play religious music while working and they don't wear clerical collars during their efforts, but their outstanding ministry to hurting humanity does not go unnoticed by our Heavenly Father.

CHAPTER 27

The Demon of Pain

As we pulled up at our home in Atlanta, we couldn't help seeing the huge "For Sale" sign in front of the house. I saw a tear fall down Dottie's cheek as we drove past it into our driveway. We were trying to sell the house because we needed the money for medical bills.

Dottie insisted on trying to walk in the house, and as she passed a table or a chair, she would pat it and thank God for allowing her to be home.

When Destiny, Israel, Reba, and Dony came over, that made the circle complete. Dottie wanted all of us to crawl up in the king-sized bed so she could touch us.

We were both so weary with it all. Things might have been different if it were not for our kids; we might have been sad about everything we'd been through, but who can be sad around grandkids? They seemed to understand that Grand Buck and Grand Dot needed to be cheered up, so they always performed for us. Reba would send her housekeeper over to help with the house. Dony became the son I never had. I saw true ministry rise up in Reba and Dony, and it was awesome. From the brokenness, I have watched God perform in them His greatest miracle, making them vessels of light.

The past two-and-a-half years have been difficult and we have not understood why. It almost seems that we have become an embarrassment to many in the church. Charismatics teach so strongly that if you are in covenant with God, you really don't have to be sick. But we have been in covenant with God all the way through this ordeal, yet God has allowed the hedge to be pulled back.

Old-time Pentecostals believe we're being tested. If this is true, we believe we have passed the test, and now God can heal Dottie.

To be perfectly honest—and this may ruffle some feathers—we are not sure about either of those theories. Personally, I believe Satan has no power except that which my Heavenly Father gives him. I do know we are closer to God, closer than ever before. He has taught us about the character of God, the integrity of God, and His Word. He has taught us how He is always the same, and changes not.

God is trying to tell all of us something through this affliction. We speak of the kingdom now, when in reality, it is just a vision that someday we must attain, but we are far from being that glorious Church without spot or wrinkle.

Like Job, we have gone through the questions of why and at times have even questioned the integrity and right thinking of God. That was in our very worst times, and it was then that God taught us about His Holiness. He taught us that there is nothing imperfect about God. He taught us that the vessel cannot question the potter, "Why have you made me thus?" It is His good pleasure to make of us either vessels of honor or dishonor.

For several months then, we wrestled with the demon of pain. It's strange how the church is geared for instant results and when we got no quick results, we watched as one by one the people did not respond any longer.

177

We've been ministering in churches for forty years and there were hundreds of pastors that we thought were our friends, who, when this happened, crawled into the woodwork. We went for two years with virtually no one except our pastor and a handful of friends to help us financially. There is no silence like that of a phone that fails to ring for days and days with someone calling to encourage you. At the end of those two years, the medical bills had climbed into the millions of dollars, and we were not only devastated but felt almost totally forsaken.

There were a few, like Larry Lea, John Avanzini, Charles Green, Bishop Paulk, and Malcolm Smith, who helped, but by and large when I sent a mailout seeking help, I barely made postage. One major minister even challenged the need. To us, it seemed terribly strange that God would trust him with millions, but the minister could not trust my integrity to pay the hundreds of thousands of dollars in accumulated medical expenses.

We had insurance that wound up paying about half. If we hadn't had that, we really would have gone down the tube. Dottie has a very few more months of insurance, but she is now on Medicare, and it's going to wind up paying about half.

Had we not been a couple who kept our bills paid, if we'd been head over heels in debt, like some ministers are, we could not even have survived this crisis. I've been very conservative, and I still am. We have to be.

We met a new doctor from Johns Hopkins named Empting. After examining Dottie and poring over her records, he suggested we go to Baltimore for treatment.

Transporting Dottie had become a real test. She could not sit up long enough to fly. We asked several of our ministry friends about using their private planes, but suddenly no one would respond. God bless Sheila Walsh, Pat Robertson, and "The 700 Club." With just a mention on the air of our need of a van, enough funds came in to purchase a $30,000 van with gas shocks to take Dottie back and forth to the doctors.

God has special doctors prepared for special tasks. Reginald Davis of Baltimore was one of these—a young black doctor we were referred to by Johns Hopkins. They called him a "miracle worker."

After intensive testing, he decided that Dottie's spine was shifting and her spinal cord was attaching itself to the wall, and unless they could free the spinal cord and stabilize Dottie's back, she would soon become paralyzed. So, once more, we headed for the hospital.

Before they could operate, Dottie had to be detoxified from the medication; so she was put in a drug-rehabilitation ward and her medication gradually reduced.

Perhaps one of the most shocking events of our lives took place there. As the medication was decreased, demon spirits, Satan's strongest forces, were unleashed against Dottie. There are a lot of sermons that preachers deliver well, but there are few ministers who know how to battle Satan in this area.

The less medication they gave her, the more the pain built back, and it became as severe as it was when water squirted out of her eyes. She became like a six-months-old baby with no will or strength to fight. Satan pressed her so much, and her pain became so terrible that the people in the detoxification lab told the doctors they could pull the medicine back no further, that Dottie could stand it neither physically nor emotionally. When they start detoxifying a person, the emotions go haywire, and you can imagine the effect of the emotions and pain combined. It was more than the human mind or body could stand.

We battled these demons through prayer. We had to pray constantly and it seemed that all hell had broken loose.

After several days, Dottie was struggling just to live and the doctors said, "We cannot put her through any more," and decided to go ahead with the surgery.

To stabilize her, they put a twelve-inch steel rod in her back and sure enough, the spinal cord had attached itself in three places. In those places it was as hard as concrete. God showed Dr. Davis how to free it and wrap the cord in body fat to keep it from attaching itself again.

Reba had flown in for the surgery and in the intensive care room, we stayed for three days and prayed Dottie through three attacks. Some who were attending her thought the three attacks were heart attacks.

Finally she became stabilized.

It seemed that every hospital, every doctor, every nurse, every orderly had a special need to be ministered to by Dottie. We always left feeling God had used us to touch those neglected, unthanked warriors who many times must not only be "medical angels of mercy" but must also stand and try to be spiritual warriors, because of the absence of the church in their areas.

Our lives will never be the same after these ordeals. We know more about spirits and warfare and intercession than we had ever known before, things we didn't learn in church but had to learn through hand to hand combat.

After three weeks in Baltimore, we headed back to Atlanta. Dottie was in a body cast and I was to drive the thirteen-hour trip. The only way Dottie could stand the movement was to take her nighttime medication and sleep as much as possible. Even driving as cautiously as I could, I still hit bumps and she screamed in pain.

CHAPTER 28

Cutting the Gloom

To ease the burden on me, Reba and Dony decided they should move in with us. Selling the house had been unsuccessful and bills had stacked up to the point that I didn't see how we could make it. It was a real blessing when Dony took over the house payments.

Not only that, but the grandkids had a way of cutting through the gloom. Even in the worst of times, those little feet running in and little lips kissing good morning, and trying to convince them that they should sleep in their own beds and not with us, were welcome interludes. They always laid hands on Dottie's back and said, "Be healed in Jesus' name!" What a joy!

When Destiny came along, here was this dainty little gift from God, so full of energy. Her favorite thing was for me to put our song, "I Hear the Sound of Rain," on the stereo, and taking her in my arms, we would dance cheek to cheek. I finally made a full cassette of this song only, and no matter how long I danced with her, she would always say, "Rain, Bam-Buck, rain!" until I dropped from exhaustion.

When Israel was born, I honestly wondered how I could love him as much as I loved Destiny. Looking at Israel was like seeing a miniature version of Dony—strong like a bull. He was always falling down as if he were a bull in a china shop and the rougher you played with him the better he liked it. Yet he was so tender and sensitive. He filled a void in our lives we didn't know was there. The love these kids have for each other is awesome, but their love doesn't stop there. They seem to have an unending stream of love and affection to spread around to everyone.

To watch them perform, to hear them at three and five quote the names of all the books in the Bible, is a blessing to all of us. Dionne is such a beautiful young lady, and quite a talented pianist like her dad. She can mimic Reba's every vocal lick. Watching their little voices develop and sometimes slip into perfect harmony, I smile and say the legacy will not end with Buck and Dottie or Reba and Dony.

One night I slipped into their room and said their goodnight prayers with them. Destiny prayed for the ministry and the safety of Mommy and Poppy on the road, and then Israel took over like a seasoned minister, praying that "no weapon formed against us would prosper," and then they sang a song together of praise and worship to Jesus.

As tears streamed down my cheeks, I thanked God for his faithfulness and again I whispered a prayer that I could live to see these seeds fully matured and fulfilling the prophecies made about them even before they were born, prophecies of their use of the gifts God has already placed within them.

I write these words especially for them:

"There is no way you can escape the awesome, anointed ministry God has already prepared for you. After great trials and testing, Israel will become a true prophet of God. Destiny and Dionne will move in true worship and praise and be used mightily in the ministry. I speak prophetically. As much as we want to, we cannot pull you from the refiner's fire and fuller's soap process that the church refuses to preach or believe any more."

When you're writing, it's easy to go from one year to the next with just a simple transitory statement, but our ordeal has been dragged out longer than this text can reveal. From the time Dottie became ill until this point in the story, five years have passed.

Not one day, not one wakened moment has she been without pain. I look at her and ask how she can maintain her sanity. I also know the answer. It is because God is our source of strength. Even the doctors have marveled because they have never seen anyone suffer so intensely this long without losing control.

We have survived until now because of our walk with God. I do understand people who don't have Christ—ending it all. I also understand the thinking behind mercy killings. God knows how to help the Body of Christ minister to hurting people.

CHAPTER 29

Back to Nashville

Bill Gaither called and told me of a special day he was having in Nashville. He had invited all the so-called gospel greats to get together for a day of singing and fellowship.

I told him Dottie was not able to come, and he said, "Then, why not just you come and be with us." I didn't want to leave Dottie for anything, but after discussing it with her, we decided it would be good for me to take a day and get away. So I headed for Nashville.

It was a day I will never forget. We sang songs. We talked of the good old days. Howard Goodman sang, "I Don't Regret a Mile," and there was not a dry eye anywhere. What a great day it was!

As I started to pull away from the parking lot, I felt God was impressing on me, spirit to spirit, "Buck, move your family back to Nashville. Become salt and light to the city and the music industry. Start a Bible study and out of it will grow a great work."

When I got back to Atlanta, I told Dottie and then Reba and Dony what God had said. A deathly silence came over them, but after praying about it, they agreed that God had definitely spoken and we should proceed.

I drove back to Nashville and talked with my former pastor, the Rev. L.H. Hardwick, Jr. You see, I believe in spiritual elder-ship and the spiritual fathers that God has placed over cities. Af-ter telling him what God said to me, Brother Hardwick just smiled and said, "This is God. Don't worry. Come on. I'll help." That was a true man of God speaking, and the only question he asked was, "How can I help?"

The five years about which I have written have been very dif-ficult for me, not to mention how difficult they've been for Dot-tie. At my lowest moment, God was saying, "There is still more required." Somehow, in the process of His time, a new adventure awaits us. Who knows, perhaps a sequel to this book?

I would like to say the transition back to Nashville in August of 1991 was an easy one, but Satan fought us every step of the way. To buy a house large enough for our two families was like having our eye teeth pulled. It was very painful financially, espe-cially when we were still making payments on two mortgages on the house in Atlanta. But when you've used the same bank for thirty years and never been late with a payment, then you can engage in a little arm-twisting and get the bankers to walk an ex-tra mile with you. During the eleven years we lived in Los An-geles and Atlanta I still banked in Nashville.

Dony and Reba bought a comfortable but not ostentatious house outside Nashville and both families—Reba and Dony and their children, and Dottie and I—live in it.

Dony rented office space in Nashville and made my office large enough to start the Bible study I wanted to do. You'd have thought that in making a move like this, just stepping out by faith, that God would have stepped in, lightning flashing, and thousands would run to the service.

Alas, Satan never surrenders valuable territory without WAR!

I was so excited about stepping back into full-time ministry af-ter five years of doing nothing but taking care of Dottie that I did not realize how near I was to collapsing.

The National Quartet Convention had just ended in 1991, and we had taken a booth downstairs with all the other singing groups. I had worked in the office and at the booth fourteen hours a day for seven days, and I was near exhaustion.

Remember that Dottie had grown so accustomed to having me with her twenty-four hours a day, she panicked when suddenly I was not there. This, along with the medication she was on, caused quite a conflict.

I felt an urgency to get on with my new ministry, and thought it should have top priority.

But on Monday following the close of the convention on Saturday night, I had a complete physical breakdown and wound up in the emergency room thinking I had suffered a heart attack.

Sitting in the hospital room, thoughts that I can't commit to paper passed through my head, the softest of which was, "God, I wish I just wasn't here anymore." It was only then that I realized how ill I really was. The doctors explained it to me in words I could understand, words like "You're empty, you have nothing left to give," and "For a while you cannot stand to have conflict; you need to feel you're in a safe place."

If you understand that, you've probably been there. If you don't understand it, just thank God.

The shock of all this caused Dottie to cut out her daytime medicine. Her mind is clearer and she is getting stronger every day. She has begun working a few dates, not because she's well, but because it was prophesied that out of the anointing her healing would come.

The great part of this is that when she ministers, people are blessed and healed, and she feels absolutely no pain while she's under the anointing. But as soon as the service ends, the pain resumes. We are convinced that He that has begun a good work in us shall perform and complete it.

The strength of Dony and Reba in this time of testing has been awesome. No one could ask for more.

CHAPTER 30

Overcoming Satan

During the past ten years, Satan has launched his greatest attack upon the Church, and these times of Dottie's illness have been the most awesome battles of all. We have become convinced that Satan hates Dottie, not because she is a child of God, but because of the gifts of praise, worship, and music that reside within her.

At one time, these were the areas that Satan himself held. He was God's archangel in charge of praise, worship, and music. Possibly he even wrote the songs he sang.

Along comes this little girl from Kentucky who gave her life in the areas in which Satan specialized, writing "He Looked Beyond My Faults," "I Will Glory in the Cross," and "We Shall Behold Him." Why shouldn't Satan be jealous of her?

We believe God is leading the Church into new areas of revelation, new areas of worship and praise. In times past, singers, musicians, and worshippers have taken their talents too far outside the Church. God is calling these talents back to the Church, even as they were part of the Levites, and they must be treated as ministry today.

God is getting ready to send the greatest music the Church

has ever known. He is greatly disturbed with writers and singers who won't talk about the blood, the cross, redemption, covenant, and His glorious victories; so He is purifying vessels. I believe Dottie's greatest music is yet to come.

Forty years of ministry have taught us some great truths. We came through the Holiness Era, a time when we thought looks would save us, and through the Tent Revival Era, the Charismatic Revolution, the Televangelist Era into the Kingdom Now theology. All of these have been times of growth for the church, but sadly some pitched their tents and refused to move when the cloud moved. We must not make that mistake again.

I have great fear when I watch God move afresh in new areas, and then watch men try to move in and capitalize on it. God is so gracious He just lets them have it. Then He moves over and starts in a new area.

Somewhere we must learn that we can't make ourselves Lord. We must make Jesus Lord. That means Lord of ministry, tithes, and offerings. Somewhere we lost track of this and have put ourselves in charge. We have made the church a series of committees, instead of moving into His Lordship.

We are constantly seeking God's glory, and rightly so, but He cannot become one with His church until the church becomes one with Him, and gives Him the crown of Lordship He deserves.

I would be remiss if I didn't say something about how the Body of Christ responded to us during the past five years. Through the first three years, it seemed we were all alone with our struggles. A lot of times, we sat and cried, "Where's the Church?" God taught us during this time how the church must reach out. When I look at any congregation now, it seems that by recognizing their spirits, I can feel the hurts that inflict many.

The electronic church has come under vast criticism in recent times and the local church has been castigated for its seemingly uncaring attitude; but you cannot put all eggs in the same basket and expect them to be just alike.

Consider these good folk who helped us:

Pat Robertson and Sheila Walsh of "The 700 Club" have been real champions. "The 700 Club" partners bought a $30,000 van and gave it to us so I could transport Dottie to and from the many hospitals and doctors she had to visit. The van was specially equipped so Dottie could ride more comfortably.

Paul and Jan Crouch of Trinity Broadcasting raised thousands of dollars by just telling of our need on television and giving our address.

Larry Lea sent us $500 a month for thirty months in a row. That adds up to $15,000. Bob Tilton sent $20,000. Tilton and Lea, both ministers from Dallas, are preachers who were the targets of an ABC-TV "expose," two fellows who helped us and never equivocated.

These great men and women never once questioned our need; they simply reached out in love.

Bishop Earl Paulk also reached out in a big way. When things looked darkest, when it seemed to us that no one cared, Bishop Paulk was there with love, with financial aid, and with spiritual consolation.

Charles Green, a pastor from New Orleans; Abner and Esther Yoder, friends from Canton, Ohio; Mark Lowry, a singer with the Gaither Vocal Band; Malcolm Smith; Billy Joe Daughtery, a pastor from Tulsa, Oklahoma; David Demolia, a New Jersey pastor; and LaVerne Tripp, a great gospel singer from California, and his wife Edith, stood stalwartly by us. Countless pastors and friends and persons we had never personally met and did not know—contributed to help us. John Avanzini, a Biblical economics teacher from Dallas, has never failed to send a monthly check; grandmas and grandpas shared their Social Security checks with us, and prisoners who earned twenty-five cents an hour, sent their love in financial form.

All of this helped and we couldn't have made it without the help of these God-loving people. But our expenses have been more than we could fathom. We tried to figure how much these illnesses have cost. We could not put an exact figure to it, but the cost has been in the millions of dollars!

I used to say, "It has cost all we had, all we've made, and all we will ever make," but I don't say that any more because God shall supply all our needs according to His riches in glory.

We end this volume of our lives saying, "God is faithful. He is still the healer, and He has never failed."

There is much we don't understand, but we invite you the reader to a special supper: the Marriage Supper of the Lamb where we shall know all things.

Epilogue

In the opening of this book, I said by going back step by step maybe I could find some answers. I have reached one conclusion—"God is still in control." I don't claim to understand His ways but He is still in charge.

We have wept many times while reading the letters from thousands of people whose lives are filled with unanswered questions such as "Why did God take my baby?" or "I've been faithful to God, yet my life is falling apart." Why?

This is my only answer. God took Jeremiah to the potter's house and showed him the potter's wheel. He told how the potter took the clay, molding and shaping it into whatever image "he desired."

While I don't believe God causes bad things to happen to good people, He will take down the hedge and use every attack Satan brings against us as a means of molding and shaping us into the image of God. Remember, God is not through with us yet. We are still on the wheel.

Even when we are through on the wheel, there is a firing process that is used to complete the vessel. Paul walked through his firing process and said, "Consider it not strange concerning the fiery trial that is set before you." God uses adversity in His purifying process.

I wish I could just speak and all of your hurts would vanish and your problems would be solved. Dottie's back would be healed and the past six years would only be a memory. I have prayed as thousands have joined with us. But I can say "God's grace is sufficient."

Our prayer for you is that you will be molded and shaped into the eternal desire of the Father and that we the body of Christ will learn how to minister to the hurting lives of God's children. God's greatest challenge to His church is still "Love one another as I have loved you."

When it seems there is no way, Jesus said "I am the way." When approached by the multitude whose lives were in disarray and seemingly hopeless situations, the Bible states, "He was moved by compassion." He then moved into their situations and healed all of their diseases. Our prayer is that we the body of Christ be moved by compassion. Then we can move into hopeless situations and minister to the hurting world and become "the Light of the World."